KNOW YOURSELF
THROUGH COLOUR

KNOW YOURSELF THROUGH COLOUR

MARIE LOUISE LACY

THE AQUARIAN PRESS

First published 1989

British Library Cataloguing in Publication Data

Lacy, Marie Louise
Know yourself through colour.
1. Colour. Psychological aspects
I. Title
155.9'1145

ISBN 0-85030-825-9

The Aquarian Press is part of the Thorsons Publishing Group, Wellingborough, Northamptonshire, NN8 2RQ, England

Typeset by Harper Phototypesetters Limited, Northampton
Printed in Great Britain by Mackays of Chatham, Kent

3 5 7 9 10 8 6 4 2

CONTENTS

Foreword   9
1. The Rainbow Colours.   11
2. What is Colour?   14
3. The Aura.   19
4. The Psychology of Colour.   27
5. Decor, Illumination and Dress.   44
6. The Many Ways of Using Colour for Healing.   51
7. Breathing with Colour.   64
8. How Do I Know Which Colours I Need?   71
9. Diet and Colour.   76
10. Numerology and Colour   81
11. Meditations with Colour.   100
References   110

How to Use the Colour Keys   111
Index   143

ACKNOWLEDGEMENTS

I would like to thank the Teachers who I have been blessed to meet, who have awakened in me a deeper knowledge with understanding of the many realities of life. And to thank Gill Wright, who is a remarkable healer and gifted sensitive, for her encouragement and help in so many ways.

FOREWORD

The first thing one can say about this book is that there is something in it for everyone, for there is not one of us who isn't, in some way, sensitive to colour. Colour touches all our lives every day, either consciously or unconsciously. We can be sitting in a car at traffic lights, automatically responding to their directions, or bathing in the beauty of a glowing sunset, our sense of sight thrilled at the experience.

What is it within the human mechanism that responds to colour? Why do we prefer one colour, or shade to another? Our colour appreciation or preference is really an expression of our intuition, and by understanding the significance of colour, we gain an insight into our intuitive senses. Why are we drawn to blue on a day when we feel agitated, or red when our energies seem low?

By studying the many aspects of colours, we begin to see that the correct choice of those we need around us can greatly improve our health and well-being. Even if we can't rush about redecorating the house, or buying new clothes, we can introduce beneficial changes each day through our food. Just think for a moment about the remarkably wide range of colours we can see at our local greengrocer's shop, the many reds, oranges, greens and yellows, as well as those from the blue-indigo-violet end of the spectrum.

Nature's cloak of many colours is something we often take for granted. Is there a particular significance in the fact that green is the predominant colour in nature? The green ray has been called the bringer of balance between the two worlds of spirit and matter. When looking at the seven major energy centres, or chakras, green is associated with the heart centre, the harmonizer between the lower and higher natures of man.

I believe that one of the great changes we shall see in health care will come in the treatment of mental illness, and that the right use of colour will be developed to provide an enhanced foundation for healing these conditions.

What we are really discussing is 'vibrational' medicine of a higher frequency than the allopathic drugs used today, which often serve to dull the senses, affecting particularly the relationship between the quadrants of our being, the psychological, intellectual, physical and spiritual.

Whatever our present attitude to the vibrational experience that we call colour, there is much to be discovered on the subject, or perhaps one should say re-discovered. The knowledge of life's gifts of healing, whether from the plant or mineral kingdoms or the realms of music and colour, were known by much earlier civilizations.

As you settle down to read this book, take note of the colour of your surroundings, of the clothes you are wearing, and begin your journey into the spectrum.

Gill Wright

THE RAINBOW COLOURS

To the Egyptians colour was metaphysical. They worshipped the sun for they were aware that without it there would be no light, no warmth and no life. They built temples of colour for healing, where people could go to be revitalized and renewed. The sun is the greatest purifier but, like everything in life, there is a balance; too much and the sun will burn and destroy.

The rainbow colours are visible when there is moisture in the air and the sun is shining. The particles of moisture act as prisms and refract the colours which are within white light. When I was in Canada several years ago, after a severe snow storm the snow froze on the trees and when the sun shone again the trees lit up like fairy lights. The melting snow was acting as a prism and radiating the rainbow colours — it was a wonderful sight to see.

The knowledge and healing power of the colour rays was nearly lost when the Ancient Greeks made colour a science only. We have to give thanks to the few who through time have passed on the knowledge and philosophy of the colours. Colour is a science but it is also a deep philosophy and the two aspects should go hand in hand. In the Middle Ages Paracelsus reintroduced the power of the colour rays for healing, although he also used herbs and the healing power of music, in fact many of the alternative medicines we know today. A man way ahead of his time, he was hounded throughout Europe, ridiculed for his work, and unfortunately most of his manuscripts were burnt. Now he is thought of as one of the greatest doctors and healers of his time. Isaac Newton was another pioneer into colour and he worked at it for a long time before he found that when looking through a prism one could see seven colours. When he tried to break them down even further he found he could not.

It is interesting to note that seven is a number associated with the Earth, for we have seven days of the week; seven musical notes in a scale; it is said that over a period of seven years all the cells are renewed in the human body; seven times four is a lunar month, relating to the woman's cycle of menstruation; and we have seven senses, two of which the majority have yet to open: clairaudience, which is to hear from another dimension, and clairvoyance, to have clear vision and 'see' the invisible world. We also refer to the seven wonders of the world, seven major planets, the seven seas and so on. Once we start to get into the sciences we realize we live in a very ordered universe. It is mankind that makes it disorganized with his behaviour. Today many more people are awakening to deeper issues and taking responsibility, levels of communication throughout the world have opened up, and more knowledge of the universe is known by those who seek. Esoteric knowledge at one time was only given out through the Mystery Schools but today it is available for everyone. This helps us to understand so much of what is going on today.

The seven colours make many combinations: add black and we have shades, add white and we have tints. Red alone is said to have thousands of different colours within its spectrum but with any colour we start with the true hue of that colour which we see through a prism. This is the colour that artists have tried to depict in order to capture the luminosity and depth we see in nature.

We live in a world of duality: positive and negative, darkness and light, hot and cold etc. The colours are the same: they have a warm and cold spectrum and positive and negative attributes. The positive attributes are the tints and the negative attributes are the shades, and the only colours this does not quite apply to are some of the greens and blues. In the green we have the strong dark greens which can give us strength and in the blue range we have royal blue and navy blue depicting positive qualities.

We are fortunate today to be able to wear all the different colours for in the past only those of noble birth could afford them. At that time natural dyes were used and were very expensive. Synthetic dyes are used today, and that enables us to have a wide choice. In Ancient Rome, those in high office wore purple robes as they knew this colour meant power, and it also represented nobility and authority.

Every era throughout history reveals the characteristics of the period through the colours they wear: when it is a time of prudence and sobriety then sombre colours are worn. The dress of the early Quakers showed their solemnity and that they lacked lightness and joy. When mankind feels free and lighthearted, paler colours are worn. It is interesting to watch the colours of the seasons and how they change in the fashion world. As I write, there is a lot of red about, which denotes strength, courage and the pioneering spirit in its positive side, but the negative side is violence and brutality and all of this we can observe today. An American lady noticed that just before the last world war there was a lot of red being worn, and that applies today. But let us think of the courage that red can give to each and every one of us. She referred to the red at that time as the War God, but she also observed that as the war was coming to an end, the paler blues were being introduced, announcing peace and bringing the healing everyone needed.

At the height of the Egyptian civilization it has been said they linked into the highest aspect of the red and yellow rays. Love is an attribute of the red ray and wisdom an attribute of the yellow ray (see the colours and their attributes). Today we are working through the green ray, for out of the chaos which we are living in at the present time will come harmony and peace. When we long for peace and pray for it, then peace will prevail. The deeper knowledge of the blue rays of the soul will be uncovered, the rays of intuition and inspiration, and we shall begin to understand the meaning and purpose of life, the cause behind all form.

We are on the threshold of a New Age, the Age of Aquarius, the Age that will become known as the Solar Age. Leading scientists will become interested in the sun's rays as oil and coal resources dwindle and a way will be found to harness this great supply of energy that pours into the earth from the sun. It is happening already in the heating of our homes and swimming pools etc, for the sun's rays can provide us with all our needs.*

There is a great interest in colour today, relating to the clothes we wear, to the decor in our homes, offices and hospitals etc, but we need to be aware of the deeper aspects of the colour rays which I hope you will find in this book. For we can then awaken in others the knowledge that colour can and does make us feel better in every way, depending on the colours that are used. We need to open our minds and our awareness so that we can uncover the deep knowledge and wisdom hidden in the divine cosmic rays that we are part of and immersed in all the time.

* See *The Splendour of Tipheret* from the Complete Works of Omraam Mikhaël Aïvanhov (published by Prosveta, ISBN 2-85566-110-2).

WHAT IS COLOUR?

We relate to the colours through sensation and interpret what we can see by how we feel and react towards that colour. Scientists are not really concerned with the spiritual and psychic aspects and look at colour only as wavelengths, vibrations and energy. We can thus divide colour into three aspects: Light, Chemistry and Sensation. Each has its own laws and unique phenomena.

The Chemistry of colour involves pigments and compounds, and the three primary colours, red, yellow and blue. We need two colours to make another colour and they blend together in the following way.
RED and YELLOW make ORANGE.
YELLOW and BLUE make GREEN.
BLUE and RED make VIOLET.
All these colours blend into black.

The physics of colour involves Light, and the three primaries are red, green and blue violet. When they blend together:
RED and GREEN make YELLOW.
GREEN and BLUE/VIOLET make a LIGHT TURQUOISE.
RED and BLUE/VIOLET make MAGENTA.
White is the unity of all the hues.

The Sensory aspect of colour is visual and embraces physiology and psychology. Here we see the three primary colours of red, yellow, and blue, plus green. They are all unique and all the other colours come from these four. They unify in grey. See the colour sheet and the above is then very clear.

Red, orange and yellow are magnetic colours. They are warming, activating and arouse one, whereas blue, indigo and violet are cool colours. They are electrical and calm and sedate one. The green ray in the middle is neither warm nor cool and acts as a balance between the warm and cool rays. The warm colours of red, orange, and yellow magnetize us to the earth; they give us our magnetism, our energy to function at this level. The red ray is known as the spirit of life and without sufficient red in our system we become dull, lethargic and slow. Our blood is affected and our balance too, as we know if we have been in bed for any length of time and feel dizzy when we get up. This is because we need contact through our feet with the earth and when lying in bed we become demagnetized, so that the life force energy, the red ray, cannot flow through us in the usual way.

We are immersed in electromagnetic waves of energy, of which the rainbow colours are a very small part. We have uncovered eight rays so far and there are 12 altogether, including radio and TV waves, microwaves, infra-red and ultra-violet rays. There are also gamma rays and cosmic rays which we still know little about, although these are becoming a source of study for many today for they hold the key to so much in our universe.

The sun's rays are not essentially warm. It is only when they hit our atmosphere that they generate heat. The earth also has an etheric envelope, which man in his ignorance is breaking up. We pour out chemicals into the ethers and it pollutes the atmosphere. Even sending a space shuttle into outer space breaks the web, the web that is our protection from the outer hemisphere. Science today is so far ahead in some ways, but we need the philosophy and wisdom to go with it, otherwise we can destroy ourselves.

Each of the colours has its own wavelength and vibratory rate, but we can see this more easily when we place the colours in a cone.

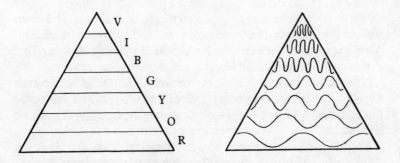

Wavelengths decrease as they rise up the pyramid and the colours vibrate more quickly

Red, as you see, is placed at the bottom of the cone as it has the longest wavelength, but it also has the slowest vibration — it has the lowest frequency. As we go up the cone to the orange ray, the wavelength is becoming shorter but the vibration is getting faster and so on up the cone. When we reach the top we have violet which has a much faster vibration.

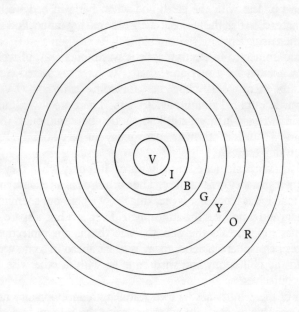

When you look down on the cone you can imagine a set of circles (see above). The centre is violet and the periphery is red. We all tend to live on the periphery of life and do not look for the centre. It is when we find the centre within ourselves that we find peace and fulfillment. Mankind tends to look outwards for happiness and only becomes more and more disillusioned with life. One will never find happiness by living on the surface; only by finding the centre will all things be revealed: knowledge, wisdom and understanding. The violet ray (in the centre of the circles) is very purifying and cleansing and helps us to reach for that which is noble, regal, pure and divine: the centre within.

Each of the colours has its own complementary colour. When we think of the red ray, we are attracting the green ray which is its after-image. The red ray also attracts the blue ray which is used as its complementary colour for healing.

The following are the complementary colours.

Red attracts Green and Blue

Orange attracts Indigo

Yellow attracts Violet

Green, being the middle of the spectrum, has no complementary colour in the spectrum and it is neither warm nor cold but green and magenta are often used as complementary rays. Magenta is created from the infrared and ultra-violet light rays, but as it has no density of colour you cannot see it using a prism (see the colour sheet). When we give colour healing we need to use colours from the warm and cold parts of the spectrum to bring balance to the system. All disease, or disharmony, that is in the body shows up as too much of one colour. It can be an excessive amount of a colour from either the warm spectrum causing a fever or a colour from the cool spectrum that is causing the imbalance. By introducing the colour required, the bodily system finds its balance again as the healing proceeds. Starting and finishing a colour treatment with the green ray brings peace and harmony to the affected cells.

We also receive the colour rays through our eyes. The sensors known as rods are sensitive to low levels of light while those known as cones require a greater intensity of light and are sensitive to colour. They also create a much sharper image than the rods. The area in the centre of the retina has the highest concentration of cones and these produce sharp colour images while the rest of the retina contains mainly rods. The retina, optic nerve and brain forms one whole system called The Eye Brain.

When we cannot see or we lose our sight the whole system is put out of balance until it can readjust. The eyes are no longer receiving the light rays, but gradually they are picked up by the skin. This can take time, so for someone who goes blind it is obviously very traumatic, but the body itself has to come to terms with the blindness and nature can then find a way round the problem. Blind people can become very sensitive in their fingertips and can then pick out colours by touching them: they tune into the frequency whether they are aware of it or not. You can try for yourself: close your eyes and hold different colours in your hands and see how many you can get right. This does help to increase ones sensitivity.

Carol Anne Liaros in the United States was working with the blind and helping them to see by getting them to concentrate on the brow centre in the middle of the forehead, to think light even if they could not comprehend what she meant. A lady who had been blind from birth practised this and after a long time found she could see through the brow centre light waves of energy around different shapes. She was told what these were and gradually she built up a way of recognizing various objects. She found street lamps easy to pick out and objects such as books. Once she had held it in her hands she saw an image of the shape of the book as light. I met them both at the Festival for Mind, Body & Spirit in 1978, in London, and it was clearly a marvellous advancement to help the blind to see light in this way.

When we look at the colours of flowers we see that they are radiating the colour they have not absorbed, and this applies in all nature. All the other colour rays have been absorbed but it is the particular frequency of energy which gives it its colour that we see, and as our own vibrations of energy increase we shall begin to see colours that for the moment are but a dream. As it is, many more colourings are being introduced today that were not seen years ago.

THE AURA

Clairvoyants throughout the ages have spoken of an aura of light around all life forms. Artists have shown haloes around great spiritual beings for thousands of years. In more recent times, we have only to look at the art produced in the Renaissance, when there was a form of sacred art. Some of the artists then were highly intuitive and very spiritually aware. In the East artists not only placed a halo round the heads of saints but also showed in some cases the aura. In Tibet they always surrounded the person with an aura of the seven rainbow colours. The sayings 'I saw red', 'I feel blue' and 'being green with envy' have come down through the ages from a time when mankind understood the true meaning of the colour rays.

Before the First World War, Dr W. J. Kilner, who was a medical electrician at St Thomas's Hospital in London, invented an apparatus which excluded certain light rays to render visible ultra-violet light. It took him several years to invent a screen he could use but he and his colleagues found that every human being was surrounded by a faint luminous mist which he said extended to about 18 inches to two feet in all directions, and was normally oval in shape. Sometimes it lost its oval shape and at other times dark patches appeared in it. He also found that by an effort of will the emanations around this aura could be changed, and those people who had a strong vital force in their energy field had an effect on a weak aura. It acted as a sponge absorbing the other person's energy rather in the manner of vampirism. He realized that his discovery could be used medically to diagnose disease, and he developed a system of auric diagnosis, but he never managed to interest the medical world. He even published a book called *The Human Atmosphere* detailing his discoveries but it seems as though the timing for these things to be known on a wider scale was premature.

It wasn't until Kirlian photography was introduced that academics and the medical world started to take an interest and investigate the aura. The Russians had been working on energy fields for many years when a Russian electrician called Semyon Kirlian discovered a way of photographing these energies. When he and his wife Valentina, who was working with him, showed Russian scientists how it was done, a new age of investigation into the aura was born. They found that when a leaf was photographed it had a glow around it but that it soon began to fade. They photographed vegetables and found that when they cut them light streamed from them, releasing the life force energy. Further investigation found that disease changes the colours in the aura and the patterns in the energy field, and tests showed that auric changes occurred three weeks before they manifested in the body.

In Russia in 1968, in front of a Soviet Scientific Conference, Kirlian photographs were taken before, during and after a patient had been given healing by the laying on of hands. The difference was amazing and the brightness in the aura increased enormously. I have witnessed this in London when Harry Oldfield carried out the same experiment on a patient and used the Kirlian method of diagnosis. Kirlian photographs have also shown the emanations that pour forth from a healer: the hand is blue but the fingertips are a dazzling corona of light.

Many experiments around the world have taken place to investigate these energies and it has been found that all life has an energy field around it. This field can vary in intensity depending on the state of the life force at the time. Photographs have been taken before and after someone has been meditating revealing that the aura beforehand was seen as unclear and not very bright but afterwards it was clear and had a luminous light around it.

C. W. Leadbeater, a well known Theosophist who has been dead for many years, produced a book called 'Man Visible and Invisible' which has many coloured plates showing the human aura as seen by several clairvoyants. It shows how we influence our aura by our emotions and thought patterns. For instance, black indicates hatred and malice,* flashes of red on black show anger, grey is shown as zig-zagged lines of energy around a person and denotes fear. Yellow, when very pronounced in the head, denotes an intellectual but when golden yellow radiates above the head it is highly spiritual and denotes wisdom. A radiant blue is devotion to a high ideal, the miser is seen as having brown lines around

*See The Psychology of Colour.

the aura and the depressed person has blue/black lines of light energy surrounding them.

The aura of a high spiritual being radiates the three primary colours of red, yellow and blue, but the red has transformed into the pink of universal love, the gold all round the head is wisdom and blue is devotion to God. I have seen a plate of an aura of a person who is in love showing beautiful colours but round the feet and the legs rather dingy shades. It is as though for a while this person was lit up: all they could see was beauty in form and their feelings showed this. But as we know, this state of being does not last so the other, everyday colours would gradually come back, although they would not be so dull as before because we constantly colour our aura with all the experiences that happen to us. The great Masters, by which I mean spiritual beings of great purity, radiate all the colours like a luminous light, going into white, and their light can extend many miles.

The clairvoyants seem to agree that this is a good overview of what is seen, but it will always depend on the person's level of spiritual awareness as to how accurate they are. The faculty of clairvoyance, 'to see', and clairaudience, 'to hear', is within us all but it needs to develop naturally and never be forced. Those who have taken drugs may have had glimpses of another reality but they are breaking the etheric web which acts as a protective shield around the body. They need a special sort of healing, otherwise they can be open to many forms of unpleasant psychism.

The seven colours we see through a prism make up the auric colours. When one is healthy, the colours are bright and full of energy but when the colours are dull they suggest a droopy effect and we say 'I feel washed out' or 'I'm off colour'. We should realize what we are saying. Eventually, when we can all see these auric colours around others, mankind will give more care to actions and thoughts, and feelings, for all will be known to those who read the aura. At the present time we often have a sense of when something is wrong, and on those occasions we are tuning into the aura without realizing it. The more sensitive we are, the more we are aware and can tune into these energies. We are so much more than it appears, we are Body, Mind and Spirit.

The Aquarian Age to come will investigate the power of the mind, for we only use one fraction of it today. The effect of the mind on our health and conditions in life we are becoming more and more aware of — 'as we think, so it is'. To prove this, write down over a period of a month your thoughts and see how they come to fruition in time, for we can attract or detract with our thinking processes, sometimes unconsciously, but we do it nevertheless. This is why it is important to become consciously aware of what we say and do. In the Soviet Union, the equivalent of millions of pounds is being spent to investigate the paranormal. They are way ahead of the West so let's hope that all knowledge will be shared and put to good use for the sake of mankind. The main development in the West is how to visualize oneself well and radiant, a valid exercise for all illness develops in the mind first of all. It has been said that 70 per cent of all illness is psychological (our reaction to events), 20 per cent is due to infection, wrong diet and lack of exercise, and 10 per cent through shock, drugs and operations.

So let us realize that everything in nature generates its own aura and atmosphere, we all possess a magnetic field of energy and when we are emotionally unhappy we demagnetize ourselves. The colours around us are our thoughts, feelings, character and conditions of our health. By using our mind with an understanding of the colour rays and linking them to the virtues, we can change conditions within us and that changes conditions around us.

Each of the colours is linked to different levels of our being (see diagram below).

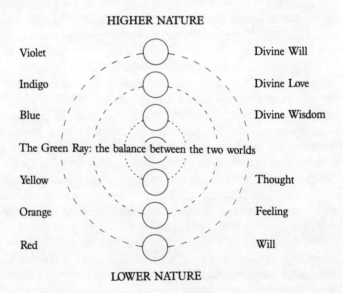

The circles represent the seven chakra centres.

'As above, so below' is a saying handed down throughout time and, as we see in the diagram, below links with above. The red ray of the physical body is also known as the ray of will and strength; its opposite is the violet ray of God's will, divine will. The orange ray is related to our personal feelings and desires, and it links with the indigo ray of divine love. Yellow is related to our mind and thoughts and above it is the blue ray of intuitive understanding, or divine wisdom. The two aspects of our natures, the lower and the higher, reflect how we live in the two worlds of heaven and earth. I recommend the book *The Second Birth* by Omraam Mikhaël Aïvanhov, a great initiate who simplified these truths for us all to understand. He also explains that by taking three sides of a prism and linking them to the intellectual (thought), the heart (feeling) and the will (action) elements we see that the equilateral prism is the symbol of the man whose intellect, heart and will are equally developed, perfectly balanced (Fig. 1). This is rare, to be truly balanced, and we tend to be represented by prisms, or triangles, that have unequal sides. Some have the will more developed (Fig. 2) which means they are good at putting into operation someone else's ideas. Others have the sides of the intellect and the heart more developed than that of the will (Fig. 3) which means that they mostly reflect and analyse, that they

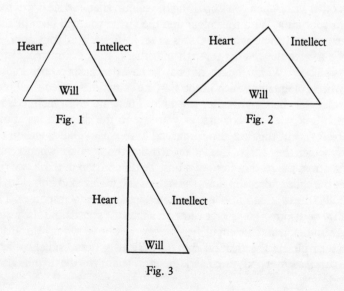

Fig. 1   Fig. 2

Fig. 3

are very sensitive but when it comes to acting or putting something into operation they need someone else to help or to do it for them.

'Man know thyself' was above all the portals in Ancient Egypt for when we know ourselves and want to change we have to have an idea of how to go about it. We can think of the individual colours, but we need to be aware of their virtues as well.

Here I have listed some of the virtues.

Red	Courage, perseverance. Goodness. Love.
Orange	Purity, holiness.
Yellow	Wisdom, discernment, right judgement.
Green	Compassion, understanding, kindness. Generosity. Humility.
Blue	Faith, trust (and the same as Indigo).
Indigo	Loyalty, integrity (and the same as Blue).
Violet	Sacrifice, unselfishness.

Wear the colour, think the colour, and breathe it into you (see Breathing with Colour). This way, after many months we find we are in tune with its vibrations. Use the virtue to go with it, and you may be able to find others beyond those I have listed here, so the vibration will stay with you otherwise, when you stop using the colour, after a while it will fade from your aura. With the colour and the virtue you will become that vibration and those who have eyes to see will see it in your aura.

We receive the colours through the etheric aura, the matrix of the physical body. Within the etheric body we have the chakra centres, known as wheels of energy, which in the East are sometimes called the Lotus Flowers, for that is what they resemble. There are seven main centres which link with the colours, as you saw in the diagram (as above, so below), but they are also connected to the main glands within the body which they affect. The red ray activates the adrenals: when a child runs across the road in front of a bus, we do not stop to think, we run after the child. Adrenalin flows through us and we respond immediately. It is also the ray that stimulates our emotions and sexual responses. The orange ray controls the splenic centre. It affects the gonads and also assists in assimilation and the circulation processes. The yellow ray stimulates the solar plexus, the great brain of the nervous system, and also affects the pancreas, liver and spleen. The green ray stimulates the thymus gland

and the heart centre, and also helps to balance our emotions to bring harmony within. The blue ray affects the throat centre, the thyroid gland, and is known as one of the greatest antiseptics in the world for it has a soothing and cooling influence on the whole body. The indigo ray is linked to the brow centre and the violet to the crown centre at the top of the head. These two centres affect psychic development and are linked to the pituitary and pineal glands.

The ancient Mystery Schools always referred to these seven colours as the Seven Spirits before the throne of God and they are known as:-

The red ray	The Spirit of Life.
The orange ray	The Spirit of Health, Purity.
The yellow ray	The Spirit of Knowledge and Wisdom.
The green ray	The Spirit of Evolution.
The blue ray	The Spirit of Truth.
The indigo ray	The Spirit of Power with Knowledge.
The violet ray	The Spirit of Sacrifice and High Ideals.

The aura is our greatest protection. We need to work on it to strengthen it with the red of life, orange of health, yellow of wisdom, green of peace and harmony, blue for inspiration, indigo for intuition, and violet for spiritual power. But most of all, think of the white light which has all the colours within it for it is the light that feeds, nourishes and sustains us. Any plants or living thing that is placed in the dark will wither and die.

The most wonderful time of day to receive these light energies is in the morning when the sun rises. Every day the sunrise is different and we know that every day the sun will rise to bring us the daylight. Let us link with the sun and thank God for the day and ask that these colour rays will lift and enlighten and inspire us. The energies at this time of the day are purer and more luminous than at any other time. Animals respect the sunrise, as observed by a lady I once met who had visited Kenya and stayed near an animal reserve. She told me that just before the sun came up the animals were silent and when the sun rose there was a chorus the like of which she had never heard before or since.

We do not realize the importance of the light and the light rays today, so many of us are focused on material things and never stop to wonder at the source of the supply that gives us life energy and growth. Mankind needs to get back to grass roots and give thanks every day for the light, life and warmth which the sunlight gives unceasingly. It brings growth, without which there is no evolution. There is an apposite saying I came across some years ago:

> *To regain the Kingdom of God*
> *We must don the white robe of purity*
> *The red robe of sacrifice*
> *The blue robe of integrity*
> *As did the noble Gods of old.*

THE PSYCHOLOGY
OF COLOUR

All nature reflects back the qualities of the colours. In the springtime we see a lot of green and yellow, everything in nature is coming to life and suddenly everywhere is so green, as the leaves on the trees start to come out.

There is a freshness and aliveness that we only see and feel at this time of the year. As the sap rises in all nature so our energy rises, we feel young and alive, there is expectancy in the air, the golden yellow daffodils in the gardens and woods also herald the spring, our awareness expands and new ideas flow to us. The woods are full of bluebells giving refreshment to our soul; new beginnings lie upon the horizon. We breathe in the fresh air and long for open spaces for we know a new cycle has begun as springtime is here.

In the summer months there is a profusion of colour, nature is in all its splendour, and when we go into the gardens the vibrancy from the flowers greets us. Think of the many-coloured roses in the gardens, especially the red and pink roses which we associate with love. The beauty, shape, form and colours of delphiniums, so majestic in the gardens of England, the azure blue colour of these wonderful flowers, the blue of the forget-me-not, the pansy with its many faces looking at us — do we stop to think of why they are so named? Flowers are a language just like colours and they interrelate. Nature is revealing itself in all its glory and, whatever part of the world you live in, the colours and perfumes at the height of the summer can be intoxicating to us all, as they are to the trees and insects. Summer months help us all to feel lighter, brighter and better in every way.

Autumn, on the other hand, is a time for reflection. The autumn tints of soft golden tones are to be seen in all nature, life is turning inwards to start a cycle again. Winter is when life balances, restores and regenerates itself and red, green and violet are very significant for the winter months. The evergreen trees act as a balance within all nature, the red ray renews the life force energy and violet purifies and cleanses, releasing that which is not needed, clearing the dross. We often see tones of these colours in the autumn and winter months in the leaves and trees as they change into red and golden hues, particularly before they fall to the ground.

Christmas is a time when the colours of red and green are very prominent. The red ray is love and the green ray is energy, or money, and it is of course a time of loving — and of expense. At Christmas we give presents to our family and friends and send out greetings of love and light round the earth. We all tune into these two colours of red and green and their frequency, whether we are aware of it or not, the colours of giving and receiving.

In some parts of the world Christmas trees are brought into the home and decorated with candles, fairy lights and coloured baubles. We are really bringing in the light and colour we long for as the days are shorter and we are missing the sunlight. Often traditions come from a deep longing from within and we try to compensate for it in another way — let us also remember we have coloured crackers for the table. It is a time of warmth, love and friendship, the one time when many people really think of others and those less fortunate. The red ray being the Spirit of Life, we need to tune into this ray throughout the year and bring love, warmth, and kindness into other people's lives.

The winter months are a time of going inwards, preparing for the spring. We see the holly with its red berries on it and the mistletoe with the white berries. It is the white flower that shows itself in winter, the Christmas Rose with its white petals and the lily of the valley, one of the first flowers to herald the spring, which has often forced its way up through the hard ground then displayed perfectly formed bell-shaped flowers in white and with such fragrance. Surely here is a deeper message for us all: that what appears as adversity is the time when we really grow within and the auric colours around us shine more brilliantly.

All life is a rhythm of day and night, inbreath and outbreath, of giving and receiving at all levels of our being, but these rhythms have been lost today and this is why chaos reigns. Nature is our greatest teacher; let us observe and reflect and work with these energies and not against them.

The fashion world has a great responsibility for the colours they introduce, for each season affects everyone. Obviously the colours for spring are lighter in tone than those of the winter months, but we need to be aware of how they are affecting us. As human beings we can complement nature — we do not necessarily have to copy nature. The three colours much used by the fashion world are black, brown and grey, so I will start with these first of all.

BLACK

Black is not a colour but gives power to other colours. For instance, when you link black with red it enhances the red and gives one physical power. Black worn with pink gives one social power, and black worn with yellow gives one intellectual power.

Mankind has never really understood black. It is associated with mystery and the unknown. In the Bible we read 'and God said: Let there be Light' — out of the darkness comes the light and the light brings life and warmth, for without light we would have no food. It is the light that nourishes, feeds and sustains all life. Take a seed in the ground, or the seed in the womb; all is darkness to begin with then, when it is ready, new life is born and it comes into the light. Mankind talks about the dark night of the soul, a period in ones life when a transformation from one state of consciousness to another is taking place, whether we are aware of it or not. It's like going through a doorway not knowing what will be on the other side, and after it is all over we literally come out into the light: we have a greater awareness of life and, for some, a deeper meaning and purpose.

Black is unmanifested light: the potential of what can be is there but it needs the light to grow. Let us remember what we associate with black: depression, a black mood, despair, black magic and we talk about the dark side of our natures. It is all that is hidden, it could indicate a secretive nature or being devious, not always being truthful or, on the other hand, a beautiful nature of love and beauty could be waiting to reveal itself. The Victorians associated black with death and wore black in remembrance of those who had died. To the majority of them there was no life after death, that was the end, but they were only adding to their depression by shutting out the world. Some people carry on the tradition today. But those who have, as it is so-called, 'died' have been reborn into the spiritual realms and one day we shall be reunited with those we have loved. They do not wish us to mourn but to go forward in life. Think of nature: nothing dies, it only changes its form. We live through the seasons and in our twilight years should link with the golden yellow, the ray of divine wisdom. Those in holy orders who wear black as a habit are shutting out the temptations of this world but sometime they will have to face them, if they have not already done so, and transmute them.

There are those who wear black in hot climates but it is to stop the heat and the glare of the sunlight, in order to remain cool. As our knowledge of the colour vibrations increases we shall wonder how we ever came to wear black. Today men are becoming more colourful in their dress, particularly in casual clothes, and this will increase as time goes on. The woman who likes wearing black is into power and wishes to remain mysterious. She is also trying to find her own individuality: who am I? But it is the colours that help us to show our true selves for, as in nature, we display who we truly are by the colours we wear.

BROWN

Brown is linked to Mother Earth. We associate brown with the things that are solid, secure and permanent. Today, as we know, great changes are happening and we have to become flexible to survive. A New Age is dawning, the Age of Aquarius, which will bring in a new focus, so old patterns will fall away. The young of today are more in tune with these energies as they have not been so conditioned as generations in the past, they feel freer to express themselves and challenge the old patterns which are now crumbling. The changes in this century are breathtaking to some people but as we go into the next century there will be even greater changes which will bring in a greater awareness of who we are and the purpose and meaning of life.

Brown keeps us fixed to the same old patterns but we must become open to new ideas, new methods and ways of doing things so that we are flexible in our approach. Mother Earth herself will go through many changes for everything is speeding up today, bringing about a cleansing and purifying process. Brown does help us to be practical and not so wasteful, however, so we should appreciate that aspect. As a colour for furniture, especially the natural woods, it looks lovely, but as time goes on a preference for lighter woods will be in demand.

GREY

Grey is the colour of self-denial, but also the colour that is associated with fear and it holds many back from expressing their true selves. Today we are immersed in fear, our fears confront us as never before. On a grey day we feel low and when people wear a lot of grey they have placed around themselves a barrier — only when they ask for help can they be released from it. As people they can seem unapproachable. Think of some school teachers in the past, or those in authority who wore grey, they often tried to put the fear of God into a person, projecting their own fears onto another.

When grey is used with other colours they can cleanse the grey colour: the Dove greys are pleasing, but if you are a fearful person do not wear grey. The silver colour, as with gold, is associated with money, but this will eventually go as mankind's consciousness rises.

The colours of the spectrum go through a 24-hour cycle. The sun is so bright that we are unable to single out any one colour from the others but it has been scientifically proved that the yellow colour is the most pronounced in the morning, in the afternoon it is orange, the evening the red ray and after the sun has gone down the colours are violet and then indigo at midnight, blue in the early morning followed by green, and then we have the yellow ray to start the day again. A time will come when we shall tune into these cosmic rays and that will help us with our work, creativity, hours of play and rest. We have lost our rhythms, for the Ancients went to bed when the sun went down and arose as the sun rose. We are part of nature and should observe how nature responds to all life.

When we arise in the morning, let us think of the yellow ray and this will help to stimulate our higher mentality, so it is a good time to deal with the business side of the day and intellectual pursuits. The yellow ray is expansive and helps to give one a clear logical mind. It will improve the reasoning faculty and open our awareness to new ideas, new interests. In the future education will be something we shall enjoy, we shall look on it as a life process, not just 'learning at school'. This is already happening for some people today but in time people will think nothing of studying complex subjects later on in life. Psychology is a subject that will be studied in depth and we shall begin to understand ourselves in a way we have not done before.

An alive mind does not get bored — we all need a wide range of interests and projects to become really involved in the life process. People in old age only stagnate when they have no interests — they must go beyond the family circle and out into the community and become involved. The yellow ray helps our horizons to expand into pastures new, then life becomes exciting and fun. If you feel your life holds nothing at the moment, tune into the yellow ray and you will find ideas start to flow to you. Act upon them, do not wait for things to happen, make them happen.

There are many different colours within yellow: the paler colour denotes a good clear mind, one who assimilates facts well but is not necessarily academic, whereas a bright yellow would be an intellect. Do not argue with these people for they have already made up their mind; just beg to differ. The darker shades of the yellow spectrum link to conceit, the ego and, of course, the yellow coward, a saying that has been passed down through the ages. When the yellow turns to golden yellow we have knowledge with wisdom. We gain wisdom through our experiences of life — we cannot 'think gold' and hope to become wise. When an experience in life is placed in front of us we draw on our past experiences to deal with the situation, and pray for the wisdom of God to pour through us to bring about the right outcome. The golden yellow arises when we turn to a higher intelligence. We all have a higher self which is part of God and the golden yellow comes when we realize 'I can do nothing but with God all is possible'.

The yellow ray has the orange of constructivity within it, and the green of balance. At the moment we are being very destructive to nature and green is the balance needed. It is time we started to act as true custodians of this, our planet earth.

After midday we have the lovely orange ray. This is the ray of vitality, movement and activity in all its forms; how we express ourselves in work and play. This is the ray of joy, well-being, togetherness, sharing pleasures, a time of constructive mental and physical energy. When we create we know the meaning of true joy: time means nothing, we are lost in another world. Ask any artist, musician or anyone doing creative work how the time flies by. So in the afternoon we should create, express ourselves from within, enjoy ourselves — something we have all lost today, the ability to be our true selves.

The orange ray is creativity and we all have within us the artist, the actor or actress, the singer, the sculptor, or the designer etc. We are all natural creators and do not realize it. This is why today there is so much frustration: those who do not use their creativity stagnate, then disharmony and disease manifest.

Three of the most important areas to work with are colour, sound and movement — these three hold the key to our well-being. Through colour we begin to understand energy and vibrations, and how they affect us and all life. Everything on this earth is made up of light vibrations. Sound, when seen clairvoyantly, is colour intensified and is very therapeutic, or can be, for it can soothe or stimulate us depending on the piece of music. Each time you hear a piece of music in future, experience for yourselves how you feel, for slow music is associated with blue and fast music with red. The high notes are light colours and the low notes are dark colours.

Dr Peter Guy Manners (of Bretforton Hall Clinic, Bretforton, Vale of Evesham, Worcs WR11 5JH, UK) has been working with sound and colour for many years, and is a pioneer in his field. Once at a festival, he asked if anyone in the audience had arthritis in their hands. A lady stepped forward whose fingers were all curled over and he tried to open them and found he could not, so he asked the lady if she would hold an applicator which was attached to some instruments nearby while he gave his talk. This was transmitting a frequency of energy into her hand. At the end of his lecture, to the amazement of everyone present, her hand opened. The energy being transmitted had released her trapped energy and changed its frequency. Sound has many healing properties which today are being rediscovered and used in some hospitals.

Movement does not necessarily mean sport, but we all need some form of exercise to keep the body in harmony. Walking is good for everyone, and one of the finest exercises is swimming. The Ancient Greeks were renowned for movement and dance, and were well aware of its therapeutic qualities. Today, sacred dance is being reintroduced — this is movement to music with a deep understanding of what the movements mean. One is using the body, mind and spirit when participating in this kind of activity. Years ago these only took place in the Mystery Schools and Healing Temples. Those who love sports are in touch with the orange ray; they like to use up a lot of energy and you will find they are only tired when they are exhausted. This orange ray gives one confidence and independence and children who like this colour usually mature early in life.

Orange releases past conditioning and helps us to let go of inhibitions. It is a good colour for mental debility and can lift one from a depressed state — it will also help to release our frustrations and fears. This ray has the red ray of love and the yellow ray of knowledge and wisdom within it, so let us make sure we tune into the wisdom aspect so that we do not become over-confident to the detriment of ourselves, for two of the negative aspects of orange are the exhibitionist and the person who is full of pride. The paler colours of this orange ray are very creative.

When you attract peach or apricot you feel a desire to design or paint, and if you like cooking you will make up your own recipes.

The salmon colour of the orange ray denotes a person who could be on many committees, perhaps to do with charities. They like to be involved with others and in helping the less fortunate, and they need to use their energies in constructive ways. The darker shades of orange indicate a person who leans on others and can be very destructive.

In the evening we have the red ray. Sometimes we see a beautiful sunset, and it gives us a warm glow inside — the red ray is renewing the earth's energies for another day. Look through a prism and you will see the red ray is very pronounced; the red band appears deeper than the other colours. We need to earth ourselves with the red ray, otherwise we can have our head in the clouds and find living on this planet very difficult. The red ray gives us courage when we feel faint-hearted, in fact, it gives strength in all its forms. When you worry a lot, think of red and it will help you to overcome negative thoughts. We associate red with warmth, it activates our emotions and sexual desires, and when we become angry we say later 'I saw red'. Red is very much the colour of life: our blood is red, heart troubles are caused by blocked up emotions and we need to express how we feel, for it is suppressed emotions that cause heart troubles later in life. Those who live alone need the pink ray of love which is within the red ray. Having a pet to look after can help as it will keep the love flowing. People with heart disorders should not link with the red ray as it is too strong and powerful and can over-activate the heart, so they should use the pink ray instead, the ray of God's love.

Red is the greatest energizer, it is the ray of our will, determination to succeed and do well. When we feel guilty we need to forgive ourselves, love ourselves and others and this will release the guilt feelings from within. I know this is not easy to do, but working with the pink ray of love will help you.

To those of you who accept we have all lived before on earth, guilt feelings can sometimes be from past lives, and they can be very deep seated. A hypnotherapist can be helpful here to uncover the reason for the guilt. The darker colours of red denote self-pity and the ruthless person who will ride roughshod over everyone. Those who have a temper should think of pink and their anger will dissipate. Love is the greatest healer, love unites and brings harmony; in the pink ray of unconditional love, loving others with no thought of self, a mother's love for her child, the pink ray is expressing itself. Often a pregnant woman has a glow about her and you will find she is radiating a lot of the pink ray.

Love is what makes the world go round, as we all say, but I'm not talking about sexual longing to possess someone, but the love that nourishes, feeds, and brings a feeling of being at one with another. The rosy tints are the colours of human love. When we attract rosy pink to us, it affects all the other colours in our auras. Rosy pink is the colour that changes human love into a pure spiritual force and by thinking of a person or a sick animal 'in the pink', conditions around them will change. When you quarrel, imagine the person in the pink and the energy will soften and the argument will stop. You may still beg to differ but the heat will have gone out of the discussion. Rose pink can transmute all negative conditions around a given situation and we need this colour very much today.

When we add red to the rose colour we have rosy red. Here the red has been purified and you have become master over all your conditions. Add green to the rosy colour to get rosy green and here the love of God is expressed through peace, stillness and tranquility. Rosy gold has a very high vibration and should be used only when divine love is needed. When this colour is poured out abundantly it will heal and harmonize all kinds of conditions and will pour over you like holy rain — this is the blending of God's love and wisdom.

Pink is warming and soothing and calms one down, but most of all the colour raises our vibrations. It is like a blessing to those who receive it and for those who send forth this colour in thought word and deed.

God's grace is an aspect of the red ray of love and will. We have to respond in gratitude with all we have, with all we are, and then the pouring of the white light enters into us through the red ray, purifying and releasing all that has gone before, enabling us to start again, aware that we are spiritual beings living in a spiritual universe.

From the red ray of the evening we now go into the violet ray. Within violet we have many tones, lavender, purple, amethyst, all representing different frequencies and different qualities. Violet itself is a combination of red and blue — it is the colour of transmutation, where the lower desires are transmuted to a high ideal. The ray is known as the sacrificial ray, mainly because it means giving up the lower personality, desires and longings, so that our soul can manifest through us and do God's will. This colour lifts a person to all that is spiritual and beautiful and when we tune into this fast vibration every cell in our body is raised to a higher frequency — it purifies and cleanses every part of our being. This ray is very powerful, and those who have a lot of violet in their aura have great mental powers, they become outstanding in whatever they undertake to do. They are the peacemakers, the true humanitarians. Mother Theresa is an example of a person who has within her aura a lot of violet. The colour will protect her and transmute the impurities around her so she can work in dreadful conditions without them affecting her as much as they would other people.

The violet ray transmutes the lower vibration into the higher. We can in our minds step into a violet flame and this will cleanse and purify the dross around and within us but we must realize the power of the colour rays and never underestimate them. Doing this could turn our lives upside down, so we must take responsibility for our actions.

The great artists were aware of the power of this colour ray — Wagner used it for furnishings in his home, especially where he composed his music; Leonardo da Vinci advocated using this colour for meditating as it increased the power to link with the higher worlds; in fact, any great artist is attracted to this colour, and affected by its vibration. All great musicians and poets tend to agree that at the time of writing or composing they were inspired by something greater than themselves. Handel, who composed the *Messiah*, said he felt he was in another world and until the music was finished was unaware of this one.

Violet is so powerful it can impel one to sacrifice oneself to a high ideal. One would find a person having to do some great deed and they would do it whatever the consequences to the physical body. Here, one could think of Jesus and the cross he had to bear.

This ray is known as the ray of kings and it carries much power in any sphere. Like all power, it can be misused but those who do so use the darker side of the ray. The ray has the blue of soul power and the red of persisitence, the two making the violet of one-pointedness. Golden yellow is the complementary colour of violet, and they need to go hand in hand, power and wisdom together.

Purple is the colour of the great orator, we see this in politics, and Winston Churchill would have had a lot of this colour in his aura. Today Margaret Thatcher is into its power but the trouble is it can carry you on the crest of a wave to your downfall unless you use the golden yellow of wisdom to complement it. The purple ray should not be used for itself in any way. These rays are impartial when the desires of the lower self have been transmuted and then it can be used for a high ideal to help humanity. The church dignitaries wear violet, and use different colours to drape over the altar in a church. At one time one of the purposes of using violet was to have power over the people so that the Priesthood did not lose its authority. In ancient times they were aware of this but

I wonder how much they realize about the power of colour today.

The dark side of violet is associated with death, whereas the true colour is eternal life. When a soul comes to the end of a cycle of experience we talk about a purple mantle being placed around their shoulders.

Lavender is a lovely, healing colour, a colour to wear if you are attracted to it. This is a very spiritual colour and indicates that you are drawn to spiritual things. Lavender as a flower, oil or incense purifies the atmosphere.

Amethyst is a colour which has depth and it's easy to see how it is associated with high ideals, devotion and loyalty. The Ancient Egyptians wore jewellery of this kind to enhance their energy, not because of any monetary value attached to it, but because they knew it would change their energy and lift them into a higher vibration. Today everything has a monetary value, but it was not the case long ago. The gem stones have properties which will raise our vibrations and that is how they originally came to be worn.

From the violet ray we go into midnight when we have the indigo ray. This is a very deep blue (called midnight blue) and is known as the spirit of power. It is not black, but one might think of it as such. A great purifier, it will clear the dross of our emotions and the mental level of our being. A very scientific ray, the ray of pure knowledge, it helps us open our comprehension and when we tune into this ray we know the cause behind all forms of life.

This ray is linked to the brow centre, the all-seeing eye, which the Egyptians called the third eye. It is the ray of power with practicality, earthing the knowledge one receives to help all life. Those who are really in tune with this vibration say very little, but when they do it is very meaningful. They are the teachers of the metaphysical sciences, bridging the heavenly worlds with the earth. When one's perceptions are opened to a greater whole, there comes about a great longing to know 'Who am I?' 'Why am I here?' and 'What is life all about?'. And when the third eye is open, one becomes a knower instead of a believer, for all things are revealed to you.

The indigo ray will work for us when we long for spiritual truths, and at sometime this happens to us all. Let us make the most of that opportunity to open our doors of awareness and perception, and as we ask we receive. When the indigo and blue rays are present at night, it is a good time to do any inspirational work, whether writing or meditating, for not only is it a quiet time for the earth's energies but we can receive knowledge, wisdom and help in all areas of our life.

This ray is the ray of the Aquarian Age, which is now on the horizon, when the knowledge of the heavens will be poured into the earth. One day religion and the sciences will come together (they should never have been parted) and science one day will be able to prove what many already believe, that we are light beings inhabiting a body, that we live within a sea of light and all is energy and vibration moving and pulsating through time.

We now come to the blue ray, in the early hours of the morning. This is associated with all that is good and true, the blue ray of loyalty and trust, and when you need faith, think of royal blue. This is the ray of the soul, the soul which has a purpose for incarnating at this time and we need to find out that purpose. Mr Beesley who founded White Lodge, the college of Psycho-Therapeutics in Kent, England, always said, 'Find the soul purpose, stop wasting time and get into the incarnation.'

Blue then is the ray of the soul, the ray that is one of the world's greatest healers. You must have blue in your aura to be able to be used as a channel for healing or any of the psychic gifts. This is the ray of peace and serenity and those who love blue love beauty in all shapes and forms. We talk of the True Blue and people having blue blood in their veins — it refers to the highest and best within mankind.

The Madonna blue is purity and we associate this colour with the Virgin Mary. This is a beautiful blue, the blue that envelopes one, bringing a feeling of protection and perfection.

Blue links us to the higher mind which is within us all and intuitive understanding, as when you know something and are not sure how. Follow it, do not question it too closely, although we should not follow blindly. You will know if it is all right, and after a while you will not question it. True intuition is a pearl of great price and it often comes after much suffering, the suffering having cleared the dross from within and around you, so that the clear blue acts as a mirror for you to see, and/or hear, rather like a clear lake. When once we are still, we can see the reflection of the higher worlds. When we look at the sky at night everything seems vast, immense, and the light of the stars shine and twinkle, saying 'We are here!'. Our souls are as vast as the universe and not just confined to the physical body; we have the ability to go anywhere and tune into anything, but we have to become like a fine tuning fork, we have to cleanse and purify ourselves before we can open to this higher understanding and knowledge. If we do it before we are ready, we can tune into the lower astral and unwanted influences. This is what can happen when people take drugs and alcohol: they have psychic experiences and sometimes these can be very unpleasant. Again I say, think of the light which holds all the colours and this will give you protection.

The blue ray is cooling and calming and it can sedate one. When we tune into the negative aspect of this ray we say we have the blues. Navy blue is a colour of being in command of a given situation, but when we think of some of the darker tones, the characteristics are of a person being self-righteous. They think they know everything and sometimes think they could have made this universe better than God. It can also mean a person who is emotionally unstable and they would then need a clear light blue followed by an azure blue to give strength.

Royal blue means loyalty, integrity and for those who can wear this colour, it makes them look regal and royal as the colour denotes. A tendency of this ray is aloofness for those who are drawn to blue love peace and quiet, they like people but in small doses, they avoid crowds and crowded places and people who are very sociable do not understand them. The saying 'peace at any price' refers to the blue ray; these people can allow others to trample all over them and then wonder how it happened. They are usually lovely people, but need to stand up for their own rights.

Those who have quite a lot of blue in their auras often can attract people who have a lot of red in their auras. They will be able to help each other but they should not live together as they will be pulling in two different directions. One is the introvert (blue) and the other person is the extrovert (red). They both need the green ray of peace with understanding.

Green can be seen in the sky before the sun rises, this is the ray of balance in the spectrum: it is neither hot nor cold; the ray that is seen before the dawn, leaving the night to itself and preparing the energies for the day. This ray is often called the backcloth of all nature, for we have so much green on our earth, reflecting to us constantly the peace and harmony which we all long for. This colour helps our nervous system and helps us to relax and let go of our problems. When you are troubled, go and walk in parks and open spaces and you will begin to feel better, and as you walk think of peace and harmony and say it to yourself. It will lift your energy.

Green is to do with how we use our energy. Businessmen and women are very in tune with this green ray — it is the ray of giving and receiving and understanding the interchange of all we do, for unless we empty the 'pot' so to speak we cannot be refilled.

The main thing is to give to others of what we can without any thought of return and, given in the right spirit, all will be returned to us and more. Wearing and thinking green does put us into the green vibration, where we attract whatever we need for our supply (we have to differentiate between needs and wants). Green is linked to our heart centre, and when this is truly open we have sympathy, empathy and compassion towards others. Green raises our vibrations, it gives us hope. Too much green can bring about static conditions of neither going backwards nor forwards, and we all need some stress to help us evolve. Today there is too much stress but let us remember that out of disharmony will eventually come harmony because we shall all pray for it. We need movement in our lives — it is like nature saying, 'Come into my green world to find refreshment, but you must not stay too long, for all life is movement.'

Emerald green is a very vibrant colour — the great Master Hermes Trismegistus wrote on an emerald tablet truths and knowledge that have been handed down to mankind through the ages, and the emerald ray is also linked with the Holy Grail. This ray has a high vibration of energy and you must be in tune with the emerald ray to wear the gem stone, for to be false in any way could bring the wearer a negative vibration. Green has often been associated with bad luck — as a vibration it is always bringing balance to any given situation and the end results may not be what the person wanted. 'Green with envy' is a saying that has been handed down through time and this is a murky green which is unpleasant. To be envious of others is a waste of energy and a destructive force for oneself, for we can become bitter and all this affects the physical body in time. We have to realize there is enough for everyone. I am aware of the present imbalance of our earth, that many starve and have very little, but when one knows and understands reincarnation, then one can see the balance of interchange, how fortunes are made in the present for the future. But mankind does not have to go on suffering for the green ray is God's love and compassion and can bring about the supply needed to change conditions. There is enough for everyone in this world, but we must work on the way it is distributed.

It is not easy for everyone to accept what I have said, but it is true and should make us think of how we need to give love to all, for as we give so shall we receive in this life and the lives to come.

Green is to do with self-esteem and how we think of ourselves. Ulcers of the stomach are brought about by always trying to create a balance in our lives when we are unable to do so. This aggravates the stomach lining, so hence the ulcer.

Green acts as a balance to our whole system and when life becomes too much and we cannot cope, it also affects the heart. Chlorofyl tablets have been prescribed at the chemists for years for heart disorders so we are able to see the power of the green ray to bring balance to the heart centre.

Those who love children and animals, always have an open house and share what they have are in tune with the green ray. We also refer to people with green fingers when we mean that plants thrive in their care.

We all need green in our aura for peace, balance and harmony is what we all seek within our hearts. Once we find peace, the peace that passeth all understanding, then others will come to us for nourishment and sustenance, which will pour through our hearts with the pink ray of God's love.

And so we have come full cycle and seen how the colours of the spectrum affect us during the day and night of a given 24 hours. Some of these hues blend to make other colours, for instance green and blue make turquoise, and some people say this is a major ray. It is certainly very cooling and calming to the whole of the nervous system. Years ago I was told the turquoise ray would help me, for turquoise calms you down and relaxes you. Up until that time I had found public speaking quite an ordeal, outwardly calm but inwardly my stomach was churning over, but after tuning into this turquoise ray for many months: wearing it, thinking of its quality and the qualities of the blue and green rays which it has within it, I was asked to speak in front of a gathering of people and found that I was so relaxed I was therefore able to express myself better. The churning inside had stopped. I have recommended this colour to many public speakers who were nervous and they have also found a marked difference in themselves.

This colour is also a brain depressant — the green brings peace and balance to the system while the blue is cooling and calming, and also in touch with our soul. It is a good colour to use in decor with a warm colour, especially in therapy rooms and waiting rooms as people will feel more relaxed. (See the chapter, Decor, Illumination and Dress.)

Another lovely colour is magenta. Here we have the two ends of the spectrum, red and violet, which make the magenta colour, often spoken of as an unsaturated colour as you cannot see it in the prism. The red ray is the ray of love and man's will and the violet of sacrifice and God's will. Magenta can lift you and improve the quality of your life. A few years ago it was a very fashionable colour and it helped people to turn inwards. There was an upsurge to find out 'What is going on in our world?' and 'How is it affecting me?' and 'What is it all about?' Many more people at that time started to think more deeply and this is where colour can have a powerful influence. This colour will help to balance our emotions, and it is a good colour to tune into if you have to organize any event. With these powerful colours within it, you have authority and can command respect, you find you can delegate and you instinctively know when a person will be good at doing something, although they may not have done it before.

Colour reveals our inner selves. When you are attracted to the strong colours you are more mentally orientated, you keep your emotions and feelings to yourself, but you have strong opinions and make them known. It is as though the colours were giving you strength and you wish to be noticed. A teacher or anyone in authority should wear a bold colour not the paler colours, for others to take notice of them. When you are giving a lecture for instance, make sure you wear a definite colour, then the audience will listen to you. If you wear something pale they will try to tune in to you and not really be attentive.

The paler colours have a higher vibration and a person who is attracted to these lovely colours needs to make sure their aura is strong and powerful. It's a question of balance, of when to wear a bright colour or a pale colour. We tend to go through life being drawn to bright colours or the pale colours depending on our moods and feelings at the time.

Pale colours for the summer months reflect the inner lightness we are feeling at the time. Also, we are outside more and receiving the sun's rays which recharge our auric field. In wintertime we need more energy and warmth, especially in places like England, to keep out the cold, so stronger colours give us strength and energy. In warm climates people tend to wear bright colours and they reflect back the sun's rays of light energy. In wintertime the light energy is cold so we reflect that back with what we wear, the more sombre shades.

As you become aware of the power of the colour rays, and tune into them more, your life will take on a different meaning. As you wear a colour you will know what affect it is having upon you and other people. Colour is a language; it is a key to who we are. Wear black and white and you do not want others to know you well, you wish to create a distance between yourself and others, and some of you will always be hidden from your own true self. Those who love wearing white are into purity in some form or another, especially if they wear it often. Then there is a tendency to become a perfectionist and friends could find it difficult to relate to you, so to wear some colour would keep you earthed and in touch with reality. Sometimes people who are attracted to wearing white a lot have a deep subconscious reason from the past, and they feel they need this white around them. White does hold all the colours but, as I have said before, make sure you feel well when you wear it, for it can make you look washed out.

Light dispels darkness, producing a feeling of safety for some and for others it is the pure essence of God for white radiates, shines and eliminates all that is dark.

DECOR, ILLUMINATION
AND DRESS

We all have a colour personality and this is reflected in our homes and environment. The saying 'The colour we choose means more than you think' is very relevant. You may say you haven't enough money to do what you would like, but we can all introduce some colour into our home which will bring a room to life. Do not put up with a colour you do not like for too long as it will have an adverse effect upon your health.

Today there are so many colours to choose from that when you decorate a room decide what you are going to use the room for, then the colours you choose will work for you. Household interiors from the past reveal quite a lot about the people who lived in them. For instance, the Victorians used a lot of brown and beige in their furnishings and outwardly they appeared very upright, strict and conformist. They had to conform to a way of life to keep up appearances and children born at that time had to accept a lot of conditioning. Here you see the brown colour and how it expresses itself, but it is to do with growth and effort — not all the energy is one-way.

When we think of eighteenth-century France, and especially the nobility, the decor was colourful and very expressive in all forms, from furniture to china to beautiful fabrics, but then the aristocracy at that time lived a so-called carefree life and there were not the restrictions to conform to that the Victorians imposed upon themselves. The colours we choose make a statement about ourselves and these colours can change over the years. Colours later on in life could be different to the ones we chose when we were younger, the experiences of life having 'coloured' our thinking.

Today we have a wide choice, in fact we are bombarded with ideas of how to beautify our homes so be careful who you ask for advice on colour schemes and make sure the colours that are chosen are right for you and are going to help you. A colour counsellor with knowledge of psychology could be helpful. When you use complementary colours together in tints and shades they can be very effective, but make sure when choosing the colours that you have a colour from each of the warm spectrum and the cool spectrum to produce a balance. Rooms done in one colour using different shades and tints, although very effective, throw us off balance when we have been living in them for some time.

The living rooms of a house should have more of the warmer colourings for they help us with our activities, and colours also influence how sociable we are and whether we are extrovert or introvert. Orange colourings are very sociable and more extrovert, while the greens and blues sedate one and calm one down and are more for the introvert.

A room for studying needs some yellow for inspiration, but also green or turquoise, which are calming, to complement the expressive yellow. Too much yellow in a room will give you a spaced-out feeling for this colour is more like the sun's colour, as we see it, and it gives one a feeling of no boundaries, so some people feel insecure in a yellow room although it is a good colour for halls and alcoves. I do not advise it for bedrooms as it is a colour that activates our minds and bedrooms are for resting.

The colours you choose for the bedroom are important and you should make sure that you find them restful. People who like bright colours and bold patterns are very active individuals who like to get up early and often go to bed late, while bedrooms that have the pastel colours reflect people who are more relaxed and restful within themselves. Bright and bold colours for a bedroom are fine if you feel happy with them but if you suffer from insomnia at any time, change the colour scheme to pastels and your sleep patterns will improve.

Parents who have teenagers wanting to decorate their bedrooms in black should know that it is as though they want to do away with everything that has gone before and they also want to hide behind themselves. Look for the reasons behind why they have these ideas, which to some people seem macabre and strange, as in fact they did to me until I gave it some thought. Hopefully it is a passing phase for after a while they can become depressed. Make sure they are not on any drugs or have a drinking problem, and think of them in the light constantly — the pink ray would also help in this instance for it breaks down hardened thought forms.

The colours you choose for children's rooms are most important, so ask them what colours they like. You will find a very young child is instantly attracted to their favourite colour. As a colour consultant for many years, I have found that when small children choose violet and the blue colourings only, they are highly sensitive and need a lot of understanding . Introduce the warm pinks and peaches into their bedrooms for this will help them to relax and they will feel more secure.

Turquoise and soft blue can help children who are hypersensitive but do introduce a warm hue to act as a balance, for example the orange tones here would be good to help channel their excess energy into creativity. Warm lighting effects in a bedroom would also have a calming influence.

At the Rudolf Steiner Schools children are made aware at a very young age of the effects of colours. They have strong, magnetic, warm colours in the form rooms for the young children and as they move up the school the colours change: yellow being used when they have more studying to do and the greens and blues when they start to develop their own judgement and have exams to pass. Children are very interested in the deeper meanings of colour so if you explain to them how colour affects them they respond quickly. Buy lead crystals for your rooms and hang them up at the windows and when the sun shines into the room it will be full of beautiful rainbows as the crystal acts as a prism. It also makes one realize we are bathed in colour all the time.

A friend of mine who did some research on school uniforms a few years ago found that those children who wore grey uniforms were inclined to be judgemental, uncooperative and their exam results on average were poor, while children who wore blue uniforms were more co-operative, helpful and their exam results were much better. She wrote to several thousand schools to compile the information.

A university in England experimented with colour when the students decided to decorate the dining room walls. They divided it into two rooms and painted one section a shade of red and the other blue, then the same food was served in both rooms. Very few students were aware of the experiment and the feedback was most interesting. In the blue room the students were inclined to speak softly, they thought the food was good and the room stayed clean but in the room that was painted a shade of red the students spoke more loudly, they thought the food was poor, and the place quickly became untidy. This proves how far-reaching the effects of colour on behaviour patterns can be.

A room in one of the natural health clinics in London was painted indigo to see how the staff would react. Some of them went to sleep while others found it uncomfortable, as though their fears were coming to the surface. This ray is a very powerful ray known as midnight blue and it is at midnight that our fears often surface (when this happens always turn on the light and your fears will recede). The room has now been changed.

Dr Schause in Tacoma, Washington DC in America experimented a lot at one time with colour and he found that the pink ray was most relaxing for patients, using bio-feedback methods to test their reactions. He put patients into pink rooms and their tensions and any aggressiveness left them, and difficult children soon responded. It has been found under test conditions that the muscles relax when you are placed in a pink room or within a pink light, a feeling of letting go comes over you.

Let us put pink lights into football stadiums and prisons as it would certainly calm everyone down and take the tension and violence out of an incident. If you use too much pink you can become too relaxed and not able to assert yourself so all is a balance. Colour acts immediately — it's not a question of waiting for something to happen, we immediately respond.

At an exhibition some time ago I saw a room decorated all in white — the walls, chairs, fabrics etc — there was no visual colour as such at all and, although it looked impressive, you would soon feel uncomfortable and unable to relax in such an environment; a feeling of over-perfection would creep into your life, and you would become out of balance. You would begin to isolate yourself from your friends, if you hadn't already done so. White radiates all the colours in a powerful way but it does show all our imperfections — we need contrasts to be able to relax.

A room decorated in all blue, or green, with white would give one a cold feeling sometimes although in certain cases blue can be helpful and sufferers of asthma seem to find an all blue room with white calming and soothing.

The green ray can make one too passive and static even when using the different tones and one should always introduce another colour from the warm spectrum. A lady I met some time ago had mainly red in her bedroom. She was a powerful woman, very definite, and once she had made up her mind that was that. I tried to indicate that red was not doing her any good in the bedroom (the colour would over activate her energies when she needed rest) but she would not listen, and here is a classic example of a colour reflecting in the personality.

In clinics and schools one can change the mood and feeling by using certain colours and patients or children will respond immediately. When we enter any building we react to the surroundings, and that is where colour plays an important part in creating the right atmosphere.

Recently, when I flew to Europe, the aircraft seats had red pieces of material for head rests. Red to the head like this is not good, it could invoke aggressiveness, anxiety or even bad temper in a person, and that is the last thing one wants on a flight. We need earth colours in the sky so we feel safe but not red. Paler tones of the warm hue with a complementary colour would go well. On board a ship too much blue is not good. The passengers need to feel safe and therefore colours in the green spectrum with warm hues could be used.

LIGHTING

Lighting is a most important part of decor, for without the right sort of illumination the colours change and can appear colourless or dark. Some firms are now introducing daylight bulbs which give a clearer light. Fluorescent lighting is not good for us and can give some people headaches, and rooms without any daylight in them need very careful lighting — those of you who have to work in offices, and buildings without daylight, should make sure you get out of doors at the weekends to replenish your aura.

One effective way of using the spectrum colours that I have seen is by having all the colours projected from behind a suspended, white painted, electric fire that was in an alcove, also painted white. The colours rotated round on a disc and were reflected onto the wall behind. When you pressed a switch the colour of your choice was reflected back from the alcove — if you felt like relaxing then you could choose the pink colour, the yellow light would bring about animated conversation and the blue light could be used for meditation, as could violet. Our reactions to coloured light have been tested and the above observed.

Theo Gimbel of Hygeia Studios produces a lamp with which you can change the colours by the turn of a switch, and it also has a dimmer switch so you can decide on your own mood and the feeling you wish to create. Therapists have found the lamp very helpful and more lamps of this kind will be produced once there is a demand for them.*

Children who do not sleep well, or anyone for that matter, could have a small pink light lit during the night — it will dispel fears and relax the body. Hospitals at night-time could consider having a pink light

*For information write to Hygeia Studios, Brook House, Avening, Tetbury Glos GL8 8NS.

in the wards for very ill patients as the warm glow would help them to feel better, whereas blue or green light, for instance, is very cold. Green light for the nurses is not good either as some of them could find this quite draining. It is at night-time that our fears and apprehensions come to the fore and the pink ray of love helps by relaxing, calming and soothing.

In Germany especially, coloured light has been introduced into hydrotherapy pools with all the different colours pulsating through the water — a wonderful therapeutic way of using colour, for colour affects us physically, emotionally, mentally and spiritually. A knowledge of the therapeutic use of colour is important before you can use it this way. Likewise, a time will come when we can have coloured showers: by the turn of a switch we can choose any colour we like. Water is very connected to our emotions so the benefits here could be far-reaching.

Next time you go into a cathedral, church or temple, look at the stained-glass windows. Recently I visited Lincoln Cathedral, which has long stained glass windows and when the sun shone through the glass it was breathtaking.

Each of the windows had been designed in all one colour using the different shades and tints and you could literally choose which colour you wished to be bathed in. Many are researching into ways of using different shapes with colour, especially the pyramid shape as this has a powerful force field around it. You can place a coloured filter shaped as a pyramid over food to keep it fresh, monks in the past used some of these methods, and when the electricity supply is cut off it could be a useful way of keeping foods. Blue would be a colour to use on the pyramid.

So next time you decorate your home think of how the colours will help you. Make it a place where your friends feel not only comfortable but where you can go in your house to be inspired, uplifted or relaxed for remember, by using certain colours you can change the mood and the feeling of the whole atmosphere, but avoid green lampshades and lighting as this colour is not good for your eyes.

DRESS

When you need a certain colour, wear it and surround yourself with that colour as it can bring about beneficial effects. If you do not like the colour that has been recommended for you, but you need it, then wear it as underwear, or carry a handkerchief of that colour or have a scarf with the colour incorporated in it.

The colours we see visually affect us, so go out and choose the colour you need but team it up with other colours — do it gradually otherwise you will reject it and just put it in your bottom drawer. I suggested to a lady that she needed red and she went out and bought herself a red suit, but this was far too powerful for her and she said she had tripped up all week when she had worn it. You cannot force yourself into a colour. The colours we feel happiest in are those that we have already in our aura, so the colour you do not like you may find you need and it will, over a period of time, change your attitudes and feelings etc.

If you are drawn to wear yellow then you feel good about yourself, for it is to do with identity and the ego. Quite a lot of successful businessmen and women are drawn to this colour — they have strong personalities and make their presence felt.

Green has many different shades and tints, and it is one of the few rays where the darker colours can give us more energy in the way of strength. When your mind is overactive, get yourself a scarf with apple green in it, use silk or cotton but it must be the natural fibre for it to be most effective. Place this scarf on the back of your chair and then put your head back; you will find it soothing and calming. I have tried it with good results, especially when my mind won't stop going round and round on the same subject and I seem to be getting nowhere.

Emerald is a lovely colour but you need to be well to wear it. So often the colour we choose depicts how we feel, so when we feel down there is a tendency to wear dull and dowdy colours. That is the time to introduce a colour that will lift your spirits and make you feel better; it will also help to change the situation you find yourself in.

Those of you who wear a lot of blue, do wear other colours as well. The warm colours will earth and ground you, but do not wear purple or violet if you feel depressed for it will make you more depressed. You would need green or pink to lift you and help you to feel better. Today there are some lovely colours in the warm range of not only pink but peach and apricot — these are warming and help us to express our creativity.

Do not follow fashion just because it is the 'in' colour — find what colours suit you and wear them. Many more people are aware of what colours they can wear and look good in, so ask for those colours you want. When enough people come forward and want a wide range of colours, not just those that the fashion world dictate to us, then we will get them. Everything is changing, but it is up to us to direct the changes.

THE MANY WAYS OF USING COLOUR FOR HEALING

The essence of colour healing is to bring about a molecular reaction in the organism through the colour rays. There are many ways of doing this, for example you can impregnate water with coloured light and then drink the water, which has been tried with some success and is called solarized water. You can experiment yourself by taking six glasses, filling them with bottled water and placing around them different coloured filters, which can be obtained in large sheets from any business which supplies lighting to theatres. Place them on your window sill in the sunshine and leave them for about half an hour (in the winter months you would have to leave them longer), then sip each glass of water and you will find the water that has the blue and violet filters around it tastes metallic whereas in the glasses that have the red, orange and yellow filters around them the water will not stay fresh for very long, while the water impregnated with the blue and violet rays from the sun will stay fresh for some time. You can store the water in the fridge and drink it when you require it, and this is such an easy way of absorbing the colour rays. The red, orange and yellow solarized water should not be drunk at night-time as these are magnetic colours and will over-stimulate you, but when you drink them in the morning they will give you energy. The blue and violet solarized water would be fine to drink at night-time, and is good for those who suffer from insomnia. If you drink the blue and violet solarized water in the morning, follow it with one of the magnetic colours of red, orange or yellow.

You can also magnetize water yourself. Hold a glass of water in your left hand and point two fingers of the right hand into the water — concentrate on the colour of your choice for a few minutes and then drink the water — you will only know if it works by trying it.

If you can, get hold of some coloured glass bottles. I have seen the most heavenly blue bottles, like the bottles the apothecaries of old had on their shelves, and you may be able to get them in your own town. When you have finished with the original contents, wash them out well and you can then put into the bottle rose water* or bottled water and place them on your window sill in the sunlight. This would solarize the water with the blue ray, which is good for bathing your eyes, or if you cut yourself and also for stings and bruising, and you can also put some of this water on your flowers to make them last longer.

Healers can transmit the colour rays through thought to another person, or by placing their hands on someone while at the same time concentrating on the colour required. You can breathe onto a piece of flannel, concentrating on the colour you need and then place the flannel over the affected area.

Another way of transmitting the colour rays is by using the Chromolight Filter Box.† This is a small box with a shelf inside where you place one or more colour filters, which are provided with the box, and underneath the shelf you place a photograph or signature of the person you wish to send absent colour healing to. It needs to be something of the vibration of that person, and then you place it in the sunlight on the window sill. You can dowse to see how long to leave it on your window sill, and this could be hours or even days. Some of the results of using this method have been very promising. When I first used it I placed my sister's photograph into the box using the green colour filter. I knew at the time she needed space and peace — all attributes of the green ray — and I waited to see how she responded. At the time she was living nearly 200 miles from my own home, but she soon phoned to say she was feeling so much better and had I anything to do with it. Here I used my intuition but you can also dowse (see, How Do I Know Which Colours I Need?). There are instructions with the Chromolight Box and 12 filters.

Distance makes no difference. A friend of mine living in America who at the time was very unwell was given treatment using the pink-coloured filter and he wrote and told me that he could see himself surrounded by a pink light, and how it had helped him relax, let go and receive a feeling of all being well. I should add, he is very sensitive and can see the auric colours around people. We tend to block our own good

---

* Do not drink this.
† Available from the author. For information, please write to BM MINUET, LONDON WC1N 3XX, enclosing a stamped, addressed envelope.

and often need help to start the healing process.

A radionic practitioner used the pink filter to help a couple who were not communicating with each other. She decided to place both their signatures in the box with the pink filter and within 24 hours they phoned to say they would like to come along for their next appointment together, whereas before they had been coming to see her separately. The pink ray will unify and help in very difficult conditions and it also breaks up negative thought forms.

The colour orange will also help with relationships. A lady I know placed her mother's photograph in the box with the orange filter to see what would happen — they had not seen each other for quite a long time and the relationship was strained. The next day her mother phoned and suggested they meet and have some lunch together. She was so surprised and delighted and the relationship since then has improved enormously. The orange ray is to do with communication and how we express ourselves; it also helps to break up some of our past conditioning.

Anyone who has had a shock needs green to bring balance and harmony into their being. Cancer patients have been helped by using the green, orange and magenta filters, but you need to dowse to find what is needed by each individual. Animals also respond if you place a photograph of your animal into the box, and you can also put your own photograph into the box and use the dowsing method for the colour you need.

I am often asked if we can give someone absent healing without their permission. We all have to take responsibility for that which we give and receive so ask the person and tell them the possible benefits of receiving the colour rays. For these rays have healing properties and they can also change conditions and situations that build up around us.

You can use crystals with the colour filters, but you need a knowledge and understanding of how to use the crystals. In this case you will need a box with a light in it and a round aperture on the lid to let the light shine through, then you can place a crystal on top of a colour filter to give a luminous light. You can of course programme a crystal this way to have the colour you want but it can help many people to see the colour radiating through the crystal itself. They are ideal for meditation, and if you hold the crystal you will absorb some of the colour ray for the crystal retains its colour frequency. Gems also release the colour rays and ways have been found whereby one can release the frequency within the gem stone into a solution, rather like homoeopathic substances. The liquid is diluted down until it only has a tiny amount of the original essence and this liquid is known as a gem remedy. Usually a few drops are prescribed to be taken in water a few times each day, and the effects are promising. Today, others are furthering the work and quite a lot of research is going on as to their properties.

Aura-Soma therapy is now becoming known throughout the world, after Vicky Wall introduced the Aura-Soma Balance herb oils a few years ago. She was already making up herb preparations so it seemed a natural step to introduce the auric colours into the herb oils. She received divine inspiration as to how to do this, but when her first batch of oils turned cloudy she was dismayed. But she made some more and the colours stayed. Remarkably, if someone is lacking a colour it has been known for them to absorb the colour completely from a bottle.

She first displayed the oils at a festival in Windsor, Berkshire, and by mistake a cloudy bottle was put on display. To her amazement a lady wanted to buy it, although she could have chosen so many of the other beautiful colours. It was then replaced by another cloudy one to see what would happen and over the period of the festival most of the cloudy bottles were sold. It appeared that people who were mentally upset, depressed or working with people who were mentally disturbed were drawn to the cloudy bottles.

In Vicky's studio, where she kept the Balance herb oils, the all-green Balance herb oil kept losing its colour. Each time it was replaced the colour went again. In the garden she had a peach tree and as it looked as though it was dying, Vicky wondered if there was any connection, so she decided to place a red-and-green Balance herb oil bottle (one of the dual-colour bottles) at the bottom of the tree, saying nothing to anyone, and after a time a friend who was doing some gardening found the bottle with all the colour gone from it and wondered what it was doing there. The following summer the peach tree was laden with fruit, they had never had so many peaches from it before, and the epicure peaches, which were normally a creamy white colour, had turned a lovely rose pink. It seemed that the colour infusion had given the tree a new lease of life.

When the Balance herb oils are shaken, the dual colours blend and then separate, and the bubbles that form when they are shaken can reveal, to those who know how to interpret them, insights about one's health, relationships etc. Today Aura-Soma therapy uses 49 preparations, developed from the original five, some single colours and a few dual-colour combinations. The original five colours were linked to the chakra system and they were: yellow over red (called Sunset), golden yellow (called Sunlight), blue over green (called Heart), blue (called Peace) and violet over blue (called Rescue Remedy).

Each of the colours is a key and has a psychological meaning for every level of our being. When you have a basic understanding of the psychology of the main colours, you begin to start to know more about yourself. The Rescue Remedy is very good for pain — on the one occasion I had a very bad fall and hurt my wrist and ankle, and my foot was swollen so that during the night I could only crawl to the bathroom. I applied the Rescue Remedy constantly during the night and in the morning I was able to walk on my foot. A bruise I received from the fall turned my hip black and blue and within two days it faded by applying the Rescue Remedy oil. This oil is good for pain generally, but do remember that pain is a warning signal so do seek medical advice should it continue.

Vicky Wall also introduced a Pocket Pomander, which has many herbal preparations in it and, she says, is reminiscent of the Judge's Bouquet from the old days, small enough to carry in a purse. She produced them in different colours and they do seem to strengthen the aura. Kirlian photography proved this by accident — at one of Vicky's workshops Kirlian photographs were being taken at the same time as the work was proceeding and those who had used the Pocket Pomanders had a brighter corona around the fingertips. Sometimes we meet people who can drain our energies, but this little Pocket Pomander will help to stop this.

People who know nothing about colour are drawn to the Balance herb oils for they love the colours, just to display them in a bathroom, bedroom, or office. They visually feed you and make you feel better. Aura-Soma Balance herb oils can be applied to the skin, or a few drops put into the bath, but they must not be taken internally. For information about Aura-Soma therapy write to Dev Aura, Little London, Tetford, Lincs LN9 6QH, England.

Colour light treatments using special lamps and colour filters should be administered by a colour therapist. In the last century practitioners had some good results using this method and several therapists still use it today, for every organ in our body is linked to a colour. Dr Edwin Babbitt wrote the first important book on colour: *The Principles of Light and Colour*, published in 1878. It is a classic and covers many different aspects of how to use colour for healing.

Next time you visit a patient in hospital and take some flowers, think of the colour of the flowers and whether they are fragrant, for fragrance is also very important as it lifts our vibrations. For instance freesias with their heavenly fragrance are very healing to the emotions and the mind, and they can be found in many different colours nearly all the year round. When you choose roses for those who are unwell, the rose pink colour will warm, soothe and relax them, but the deep red roses are too powerful and will over-stimulate a patient. Yellow daffodils or yellow chrysanthemums are good for a person who is getting better because the yellow ray stimulates them and brings a feeling of sunshine into their room.

Blue hyacinths cleanse and purify an atmosphere, apart from giving off a heavenly smell, and lily of the valley also cleanses a place and lifts the vibrations. So next time you choose flowers, think of the appropriate colour and be aware of the fragrance. All sick rooms need cleansing and flowers are not only lovely to look at but can clear a room of impurities.

There is more to putting flowers onto a grave than perhaps most people realize as although flowers are for remembrance they will also cleanse any area that has a negative vibration. A cemetary is a place of much sadness for some people and flowers, incense and perfume all cleanse and lift the vibrations. Perfume manufacturers have a great responsibility, whether they are aware of it or not. Most perfumes that are made today are made with the intent of arousing one sexually, whereas the healing potential of fragrance has been known throughout time. Most of us can remember a perfume and its associations from the past, and if the association was good we like it, if it links us with unhappy times we do not, although there may be nothing the matter with the fragrance itself.

Even coloured candles can hold a message for us — red is for protection, orange is for travel, yellow for ideas, green for abundance and blue for healing, so next time you choose a candle think about the colour and it could help you.

A time will come when everyone will be aware that each day has its own colour, and also they are linked to the planets:

Monday is Moon day and the colours are silver and violet.
Tuesday is Mars day and the colour is red.
Wednesday is Mercury day and the colour is yellow.
Thursday is Jupiter day and the colour is blue.
Friday is Venus day and the colour is green.
Saturday is Saturn day and the colour is indigo.
Sunday is the Sun day and the colour is golden orange.

In ancient times the colour of the day was worn for that day, so that one would remember its quality and significance. At the Fraternité Blanche Universelle in the south of France and throughout their centres, the brothers and sisters wear some apparel that is the colour of the day, so you know whether it is a Monday or Thursday etc, but more important is that you are aware of the energy of the day and how you can tune into its vibrations. In times to come, as our awareness grows, we shall want to be in harmony with the earth and the cosmos.

Let us also be aware that precious and semi-precious stones transmit energies, and that the colour of the stone is important for us. In ancient times people wore jewels for healing and protection, not just for adornment, and each of the stones resonates with its colour ray. When you know the quality of the colour, you can tune into its good attributes and they will help you:

The red ray gem stone is the ruby, the stone of protection, and it drives away sadness and melancholy.

The orange ray is the pearl, which gives strength and purity and will clear the mind. Think of how the pearl is formed under great stress, but it forms a 'pearl of great price', as the saying goes.

The yellow ray gem stone is coral. This stone promotes brilliance and excites the nerves — coral also protects energy from misfortune.

The green ray gem stone is the emerald, which promotes friendship and is good for any diseases of the heart — it also links you into the energy of abundance.

The blue ray gem stone is the sapphire, which expels fear and brings joy and peace.

The indigo ray gem stone is the diamond, the hardest known gem stone of them all. The diamond stands for purity but it reflects back to the wearer exactly what they are — if they are into purity it will reflect that quality but if the person is mean it will reflect that quality. It enhances the qualities we have within us.

The violet ray gem stone is the amethyst. This stone is associated with high ideals and links us to the highest — its quality is one of reverance for all life.

I have here devised a list of personality types and which colours will help them. If you feel they might help, you can wear the chosen colour or buy something that you can look at constantly. Just being aware that you need the colour means you will find that you start to attract that colour to you.

COLOURS AND THE
—— PEOPLE THEY CAN HELP ——

Types of people	Colour
Dark complexion, eyes and hair, tend to have poor circulation.	Red
Fair complexion, can suffer from depression or pessimism.	Yellow
Autistic children and adults.	Pale Orange
Aggressive, argumentative and violent people.	Pink
Excitable.	Turquoise
Over-anxious or nervous.	Green
Lymphatic and melancholy.	Red, Green, Yellow
Consumptive and anaemic.	Red
Sanguine people.	Blue, Green
Lethargic, dull and slow.	Red, Orange
Feeling low and sluggish.	Yellow
Mental and emotional depression.	Green
Insomnia and over-tiredness.	Blue or Indigo
Over-stimulated.	Violet or blue
Cannot cope with life.	Turquoise or Pink
Mental debility.	Orange

SOME WAYS OF USING
———— THE COLOUR RAYS ————

THE RED RAY

This is the greatest energizer of all the rays, and it needs to be used with caution by those who have had heart trouble of any kind. When in doubt, do not use red. The red ray affects the root centre at the base of the spine — it is from the red ray that we get our energy — and it also stimulates the sex glands. When this centre is stimulated it causes adrenalin to be released into our blood stream. It also affects our blood cells and has a very positive effect on our blood. Whenever you are cold, think of red and it will raise your body temperature.

Red's complementary colour is blue.

Some therapeutic uses of the red ray

Affects the muscular system.
Stimulates the sensory nerves.
Affects the adrenals and releases adrenalin into the body.
Good for circulation deficiencies.
For cold hands and feet, wear red gloves and socks.
When you feel you have no energy, feel dull and slow use red.
Helps with colds.
Anaemia.
This ray can help with sexual impotence.
Do not use this ray for inflamed conditions — use blue — and do not use in cases of emotional disturbances.

The above are guidelines as to how to use the red ray to start with. There are many more ways of using this ray, and the other rays I have mentioned, but you will need the help of a colour therapist if you want to treat any major ailment.

THE ORANGE RAY

The orange ray stands for vitality and enthusiasm. Those who love orange love life and, although there are many people who do not like this colour, we all need it. Orange is a most wonderful antidote for depression, loneliness and tiredness, for orange is a mental stimulant.

The orange ray affects the splenic centre and has a lot to do with our circulation process; it can also activate the adrenals, as does the red ray. The orange ray, when used in a pale tint, has a high vibration and means purity. It can transmute sexual energy of physical desires and repressions into thinking, so that we can become creators at another level.

Orange's complementary colour is indigo.

Some therapeutic uses of the orange ray

Affects the circulation system.
Vegetarians needs this colour to give them energy.
Helps with cramps and spasms.
Chest conditions.
Chronic rheumatism and asthma.
Inflammation of the kidneys.
Gallstones.

Some digestive disorders.
Raises the pulse rate but not the blood pressure.
Depresses the parathyroid.
The orange ray recharges the etheric body which is the matrix of the physical body.

The orange ray will release inhibitions and give you a sense of freedom from limitations. If you are one of those people who do not like orange, introduce it with one or two items perhaps in the kitchen, for it can change your life.

THE YELLOW RAY

The yellow ray affects the solar plexus. Here we can accumulate a lot of negative energy, and it is in this area that we know if something is right or not — it's called the brain of the nervous system. Our feelings and mental reactions affect the solar plexus; when we are stressed we either over-eat or do not feel hungry. To relax this area, put your feet into fairly hot water at night before you go to bed, imagine all the stress of the day pouring into the water — try it and you will find you feel a lot better.

Yellow's complementary colour is violet.

Some therapeutic uses of the yellow ray

Activates the motor nerves.
Affects the nervous system.
Acts as a laxative when you use solarized water (for diarrhoea use blue or indigo).
Stimulates the flow of bile.
Activates the lymph glands.
Helps with elimination of calcium and lime deposits in arthritic conditions.
Can be used as a weight corrective.
For skin ailments.
For nervous exhaustion.
Do not use the yellow ray for a nervous breakdown, use blue and green.

THE GREEN RAY

The green ray affects the heart centre and the thymus gland. When you have been through a very upsetting time you will not like green, and the green ray is very much to do with how we feel about ourselves.

Green is soothing and relaxing, and when you feel unwell walk in the woods and parks and if it is winter go near the evergreens for they will give you energy. You can stand with your back against a tree, preferably without your shoes on, and place your left hand onto the tree trunk and your right hand onto your solar plexus. Breathe in the life force from the tree, ask the tree to give you energy and thank the tree before you leave. Try it, for you will find your energy rises and you will feel better.

Green's complementary colour is magenta (this ray has no true complementary colour as it is the middle one of the seven colours in the spectrum but it can be used with magenta).

Some therapeutic uses of the green ray

Affects the digestive system.
Relieves tension.
Stimulates the pituitary gland.
Good for shock.
Helps to alleviate headaches.
Neuralgia.
Controls blood pressure (light green for high blood pressure, dark green for low blood pressure).
Relaxes the heart.

The green ray is the harmonizer of all the rays and we all need some green in our auras to bring us peace, balance and harmony.

THE BLUE RAY

The blue ray is one of the greatest antiseptics in the world. We talk of the healing blue waters and blue affects the throat centre and the thyroid gland. It is one of the most powerful centres, for it is through the throat centre we express ourselves — words carry power.

Blue's complementary colour is red.

Some therapeutic uses of the blue ray

Affects the respiratory system.
Calms down the mind and nerves.
Good for throat conditions.
Stings, itches, bruises.
Insomnia.
Painful menstruation.
Inflamed eyes.
Teething troubles.
Shock.

When you have a fever, the blue ray will cool you down; a blue light can be helpful when a person has measles, chicken pox or mumps (it depends on how poorly they are but you can certainly use it in the early stages) and blue solarized water can be used to cool a high temperature.

THE INDIGO RAY

The indigo ray is midnight blue. This ray removes fear: if our fears rise to the surface, the indigo ray can clear the dross within us, but we have to allow this to take place. This is the ray of 'letting go and letting God', knowing all is well and trusting the outcome.

The indigo ray affects the brow centre, called the third eye, and when this is open we can see clairvoyantly into other dimensions. It affects the pituitary gland in the body, which is a master gland. This ray brings a longing for truth and to unravel the unknown.

Indigo's complementary colour is orange.

Some therapeutic uses of the indigo ray

Affects the skeleton.
A great purifier of the blood stream.
Depresses the nerves and lymphatics.
Depresses the cardiac system.
Acute rheumatism and arthritis.
Varicose veins.
Insomnia.
Boils, ulcers.
Eczema, bruising.

Indigo heals the etheric body which is the matrix of the physical body and it removes pain, but remember pain is a warning signal that something is wrong, so do seek qualified medical advice should it continue.

THE VIOLET RAY

The violet ray is the highest vibration within the rainbow colours (ultra-violet rays are of another order beyond the visible spectrum). Many people cannot cope with violet as it has such a high frequency of energy. It purifies everything within its wake, thoughts, emotions, and has a very positive effect on the molecular structure of the body. Place anyone into a violet light who does not use their creative energy and they will become very frustrated and eventually ill. This is truly a creative ray and when in tune with it, the pathway of light, love and peace lies ahead for you. Only a few people have the violet ray in the auric field as it is the ray of dedication and service to a high ideal. Linked to the crown centre and the pineal gland, this ray affects all the chakra centres and the endocrine glands.

Violet's complementary colour is yellow.

Some therapeutic uses of the violet ray

Mental and nervous disorders.
Emotional disturbances if excessive.
Maintains the potassium balance in the body.
Controls excessive hunger.
Sedates one and subdues.
Purifies the system.
Do not use this ray when you are depressed. You can use green or blue.

Important note
With major ailments it is dangerous for those unqualified to try to do their own diagnosing and treating. Always consult a qualified colour therapist.

BREATHING
WITH COLOUR

Respiration controls the quality of our vitality and our life and yet it is something we take for granted. When we are born we take our first breath and when we die we give out our last breath — we can live for a short time without food and water but not without air — to breath is to have life and it sustains us on every level of our being. To recharge our energies we need to concentrate on the in-breath and for relaxation concentrate on the out-breath — yawning relaxes us and gives us a feeling of letting go.

When we use our minds with the breath of life we can change conditions within and around us, by thinking of a positive attribute or affirmation and breathing it into our being. It has the effect of changing our energies, in the same way that we can breathe out any negative energy, like stress or pent up emotions. The longer we breathe in a thought, the longer it will stay with us and have an effect within us — the same applies to the out-breath, the longer we breathe out stress and pent up emotions the more we shall relax. Whenever anyone is upset we always suggest they take some deep breaths, and this gives them energy and at the same time releases emotion so that they begin to feel better.

When we are at the sea we tend to breathe more deeply to fill our lungs with fresh air. Water is very purifying and cleansing to our emotions, and we can use many methods using the breath, especially when we are by the sea. When the sea is calm, breathe in and out as the water laps onto the beach — you can do it to the rhythm of the waves. When the sea is rough one can sometimes see tiny globules of light on top of the waves, rather like electricity. This has the effect of recharging our energies. If you cannot see the globules of light, be aware of them and imagine breathing this light into your being. When we use the mind with the breath this way it has a most powerful effect.

We can cleanse negative feelings and thoughts by breathing in the light and breathing out all that is negative, harmful and impure. Water is linked to the blue ray — either see or think of a beautiful blue sky, and with the palms of your hands facing upwards imagine the blue rays pouring into you through your fingertips, up your arms and into the solar plexus and circulating round the body. You can use this method when the sea is calm, breathing in the blue ray with the light and this will purify, cleanse and uplift you on every level of your being. When the sun is shining on the water, breathe in the dazzling light rays that are reflected back to you. The solar plexus collects so much impurity every day of our lives that we need to release this. If you do not live by the sea then use your thought by breathing in peace and breathing out stress. For peace you can imagine the green or blue rays.

We have to use our conscious mind for these ways to be effective — the sun can warm and relax us but it is by thinking of the benefits we are receiving that we actually receive them in abundance. The potential of the mind has yet to be properly investigated for it is our most powerful tool.

Water is very healing and this applies whether you are at the seaside or by a river, lake or stream. Having a bath cleanses all our negativity (imagine all your cares and worries going down the plug hole) and here you can think of the water as any colour you think you need.

Should you happen to live near a weir or a waterfall, the water cascading over the fall will cleanse and recharge your energy, particularly the solar plexus area, and you should imagine a golden yellow light pouring into this part of you. In the same way, when you are in a wood, park or open fields breathe in the green ray. Here you have many different colours to choose from — the paler green will lift you spiritually and the darker greens will give you strength, so breathe in the colour of your choice. Some of you may feel a tingling sensation and this is giving you new life. Green is peace and as you breathe in the green ray say to yourself, or out loud if you are on your own, one of the positive attributes of this ray. Think of its quality and breathe it in to you and then breathe out its opposite — here you are transforming yourself; for instance, breathe in harmony and breathe out disharmony. Do this often and over a period of time you will begin to incorporate the quality within yourself. Generosity is one of the green ray's attributes which we can all tune into — this is the ray of abundance and plenty and we have only to look around us to see this is so.

Choose a flower that has a colour you feel drawn to and hold it in your hand. If it has a fragrance, inhale the perfume from the flower and observe the shape, then breathe in this colour and think of its qualities or a quality that you feel you may need. Hold your breath for a moment and exhale. A pink rose with a fragrance would be soothing and relaxing. Look at the rose, breathe in the fragrance and the colour and then close your eyes and try to imagine the flower and the colour in your mind's eye through the third eye in the brow centre. Do not worry if you cannot do this: just think of the flower and the colour then open your eyes. Repeat the process three times. The colour will start to impregnate your aura and you will feel warm. Your heart will relax as the pink infils and enfolds your auric field. People who are lonely or unhappy will find this very beneficial, for it will have a good effect upon them. You can use any flower with the colour of your choice in the same way.

Breathing is nourishment. Most people are shallow breathers so they are not receiving the substances they need from the prana in the atmosphere. We should all become more conscious of our breathing. The early morning is a good time to take in some deep breaths, preferably by an open window. In yoga, students practise breathing techniques, with the aim of relaxing and then energizing their energies. A method used at the Fraternité Blanche Universelle in France is as follows: Begin by closing your left nostril and breathe in deeply through the right nostril while you count to four, then hold your breath to the count of 16, close your right nostril and breathe out through the left nostril to the count of eight. Then you begin again, starting with the right nostril closed, breathe in through the left nostril to the count of four, hold your breath to the count of 16 and then breathe out to the count of eight. You do this six times for each nostril although, once the exercise is easy for you, you can double the time for each movement, counting eight, 32 and 16, but do not go any further than that and never force anything. A book called *Respiration: Spiritual Dimensions and Practical Applications*, published by Prosveta Editions, gives further information, for those interested. This method can be used with a colour, thinking of its attributes or with an affirmation, or by breathing in the light and breathing out any negativity.

You can also breathe a colour into you and breathe the colour out into the room. This is a good way of cleansing and releasing negative energy, for intance at the end of a tiring day you could try this method and it will take away the tensions and stress of the day. Next time you are in pain, think of the blue ray and imagine it pouring into your fingertips, then place your hands over the painful area and breathe in the colour through your hands. If the pain continues then do seek medical advice.

Breathing exercises are excellent for concentrating and balancing the mind. All the great yogis in India can control their breath and perform amazing feats to prove it, but we can in our own way release and energize ourselves through breathing correctly, taking a deep breath and imagining the lungs filling up to the top with fresh air, the diaphram being pushed down and then letting all that air out very slowly, otherwise we do not receive the benefits of the pure air. Always link a thought with colour — whether sitting or walking you can breathe in pink, think love and breathe out fear; breathe in orange for joy and breathe out sadness; breathe in blue for trust and breathe out distrust.

Using our minds with the breath we can transform conditions around us and within us. Breathing in the white light until we feel as though we are lit up will disperse the darkness around and within us, and we can do this wherever we are, on a train, bus or aeroplane. We are immersed in fear today: fear of losing our jobs, our homes, or of catching diseases. We have only to read a newspaper to be depressed by the bad news of rape, murder and war. We should try to avoid tuning into all of this for it does pull our vibrations down. The antidote to fear is love — the pink ray that heals and unifies all life and brings a feeling of well-being that we all need — so use this to combat fear in your life.

Whenever you feel tense breathe in the green ray of peace and harmony, feel it pour into every part of your being, saying the words peace and harmony then breathe out disharmony and you will find that conditions around you will change.

We can also use colour for absent healing. If you are not sure what colour the person needs, you can dowse using a pendulum, or place them in the light for their highest good: the white light which holds all the colours. Breathe forth the white light or colour to that person and the energy sent forth in this way will become very powerful. If you can get the co-operation of the person who needs the healing, get them to think of a certain colour and/or a white light, and thinking of a flower of that colour would also help. This would enhance the healing process but it still works even if they are unaware of someone sending them colour rays for we are bathed in the colour rays all the time and the power of the mind to transmit energy is widely known — it is only when that person blocks it that they will not receive the benefit.

The following are colour ray affirmations which you can use either in the early morning, midday or early evening — they are the best times.

Do realize we are linking with cosmic energies and that the colours work through the glandular system and through the etheric body. One is working on the mental plane to receive and transmit these energies. You need to breathe the red, orange, and yellow rays up through the soles of the feet to the solar plexus and imagine the colour pouring into the whole of your being. The blue, indigo and violet rays you should breathe in through the top of the head, known as the crown centre, to the solar plexus and then imagine the colour pouring through the whole of you. The green ray should be breathed in horizontally to the solar plexus and you should see or imagine the colour infilling and enfolding every part of you. Red, orange, and yellow work on the physical and emotional levels of our being whether it be our health, vitality, prosperity or well-being. Green is the balance for all the colours, and blue, indigo, and violet link us to the heavenly worlds as they are the spiritual colours.

COLOUR AFFIRMATIONS

Concentrate on the affirmation and say it seven times, then close your eyes and think of the essence of the affirmation and imagine the colour pouring into you, filling every part of you.

ROSE RED

This ray is stimulating and uplifting, good for depletion and it will purify the blood.

The rose red ray is pouring into my bloodstream, giving me new life and courage for all I have to do.

ORANGE

This ray is stimulating and freeing to the emotions, and gives us vitality and a feeling of well-being.

The orange ray fills me with vitality and joy, recharges my etheric body, and rejuvenates every part of me.

YELLOW

This ray is illuminating, gives energy to the solar plexus that can soon be depleted, is good for depression and loneliness, and acts on the nervous system.

The golden yellow ray fills my being with sunshine, God's wisdom and love pour into my body, mind and soul.

GREEN

This ray enters horizontally through the solar plexus, it helps the nerves and gives a feeling of peace and well-being.

The green ray flows in through my heart, bringing peace and harmony to every part of my being.

BLUE

This ray is cooling, calming and relaxing to the mind and body so think of this colour when you are ill, for it is very healing and will clear impurities.

The blue ray calms my mind and brings healing to all my cells and organs within my being.

INDIGO

The ray of power with knowledge, this ray enters through the crown centre, as does the blue ray. Opens the mind for those who seek knowledge.

The indigo ray links me to knowledge and understanding that will help me at this time.

VIOLET

The ray of purification and sacrifice, this clears away anything that is harmful.

The violet ray clears the dross and purifies my being as it flows into my glands, bringing me new life and energy.

I suggest you use one or perhaps two of the above affirmations at one time, but do bear in mind they are only ideas for you to work with and after a while you will find your own way of expressing these cosmic rays.

I quote here a universal affirmation which can be said often, for it helps us to be aware of the divine cosmic energies that infil and enfold our entire being, the Earth and the cosmos.

I am surrounded at all times by cosmic healing rays and I wish to become fully receptive to them.

Do remember, however, that the red ray is very powerful and to think of rose pink if you have any heart trouble. An affirmation for each of the pink, turquoise and magenta rays would be:

PINK

The ray that is warming, soothing and relaxing.

The rose pink ray is circulating throughout my whole system, revitalizing my cells and filling me with God's love.

TURQUOISE

The ray that calms the mind and is cooling to the nervous system. The two colours of blue and green that make up this ray are beneficial to us all: peace, harmony and balance.

The turquoise ray brings peace and calms my mind and emotions, and I am in command of the situation.

MAGENTA

The ray that is spiritually uplifting and raises your vibrations: a colour that commands respect. This ray has red and violet within it.

The magenta ray is healing my body, mind and emotions and bringing me a deeper understanding of all my affairs. I go forward knowing all is well.

When we get up in the morning let us thank God for the day and not only ask for guidance and strength to fulfil our tasks but let us ask also for understanding to cope with unexplained events. We should trust and know there is a divine pattern for us all, live each day to the full, for yesterday has gone and tomorrow is not here, and constantly surround ourselves with Light, which will help us all. As we go on into the Aquarian Age and our awareness grows we shall know the importance of the light rays for they feed, nourish and enlighten, and it's up to us to tune into them and to be aware that we are made up of pulsating light energy. *Do not do these colour affirmations before going to bed as they may over-energize you.*

HOW DO I KNOW WHICH COLOURS I NEED?

The main thing here is to be consciously aware that you need a certain colour and then you will start to attract it to you. Eventually you will be surprised how much there is of that colour around but you hadn't realized it before.

We can dowse using a pendulum to find out what we need. Pendulums come in many different sizes and shapes, but make sure you programme it before using it. Ask yourself within what would be the right movement, for instance the pendulum could rotate clockwise for yes, anti-clockwise for no and move backwards and forwards for do not understand — you should decide for yourself before commencing. Not everyone is able to work with a pendulum but do try it and see. We can dowse to find out if we are allergic to certain foods or clothing, or to find minerals in the ground, as well as to find out what colour we need.

You have to be very clear and precise when you ask your questions. When we dowse we are tuning into the right brain, the intuitive side of ourselves. It is the left brain that analyses and reasons about everything, and that makes us doubt our intuitive faculty. If you are already intuitive then rely upon that, for pendulums are only tools and by relying upon them we can lose our own ability to tune into a higher aspect of ourselves which knows all there is to know. Some people have such sensitive hands they have only to touch an object or run their hands over the colours to know the colour they need — we must remember we are all so different and there are a hundred and one ways of doing anything.

Do not force yourself into wearing a colour you do not like for you will only end up putting it in the bottom drawer and leaving it there. It has to be a gradual process of adjustment over a period of time. The colours we wear next to our skin are important, so think about it if you are a person who wears black. White radiates all the colours and pink is very soothing. If you need red and do not like wearing it, you can always wear it as clothing underneath your outer apparel so it is not seen. The energy of the red vibration will still be affecting you.

It is interesting for us to see why we do not like a colour for this can also tell us a lot about ourselves, especially when we know the positive and negative attributes of that colour. We have to be true to ourselves and maybe, for once, admit our faults. We would then know that we are tuning into a darker aspect of that colour, although sometimes we may need a darker shade to give us some of the strength of that colour ray. This could apply to the green ray and the blue ray, with navy blue and royal blue, and dark grass greens.

The orange ray seems to give people more trouble than any of the others. It is the most expressive and outgoing, and very stimulating. We all need some orange in our aural field, and those who suffer from circulation problems particularly need this colour. This beautiful ray will free us from past conditions and give us a sense of freedom from within, and it releases that which we hang on to. We may think we need something only to find it was holding us back, but even when you tell a person what this ray will do for them they still do not like the orange colour. This colour links to the pearl and when we think of how a pearl was formed through a small piece of grit being constantly agitated until the oyster forms the most perfect round-shaped pearl, perfection and purity in manifestation, we can see an association with the orange ray, when we truly are at one with it, which also transforms our own energy into a higher vibration.

For the majority at the moment this ray is used for activity, sports, pleasure and we all need some of these things, but we are spiritual beings inhabiting a physical body and can become amazing creators, each in our own right, once we tune into this vibration. Instead of using our creative energy solely for sexual pleasure, we can begin to use this same energy for doing marvellous things, as yet undreamt of. The red and orange rays are very much linked into our sexual energy and are used for procreation, but let us never forget that we can create on many levels, as many are finding out through the power of thought. Everything that happens has been a thought or an idea at some time, so think inspiring thoughts and feed them and nourish them then they will manifest for you and give you a sense of joy that other things cannot give you.

Today so many people are tired, worn out, they have no energy, but it is the wrong use of energy that is doing it. We need to recharge our batteries, not drain them, and it is the orange ray that will and does recharge the etheric field. All disease manifests in the etheric first of all but, in time, when many can see this field of energy for themselves or through Kirlian photography, we shall truly be into preventive medicine. By recharging this field with colour, with electro-magnetic energy in all its forms, we can prevent disease from manifesting in the body itself.

Those of you who like wearing a lot of blue should be sure to add some warm colours to your wardrobe, for this colour tends to make us aloof and withdrawn. Everything in life is a balance, or should be, and wearing too much of any one colour is not good for us. Colours that do not suit you are the colours that clash with your aura. When you feel good in a colour, it is blending with your aura, for you are radiating out your true colours. We need to develop our colour sense for it has such an effect upon our well-being.

You may find that at different times in your life your colour preference changes. Be aware that it is your vibration that has changed; you now like to do other things as your interests and outlook may have altered and this will affect your aura — the colours around you and within you — and therefore your choice of colours that you surround yourself with.

As children we knew what colours we liked, and parents should listen to their children and ask them what are their favourite colours. They will soon tell you. There was a specific reason for putting babies into pastel colours that today is lost: their aura is very pale and to introduce strong colours gives a baby too much too quickly. I'm not surprised that children are so wide-awake and into everything these days for they are being stimulated at such a pace. Each stage has its time: in the very early years a child needs love, comfort, and to know they are wanted more than anything else — this is the foundation that builds a happy child and adult. The colours you give your baby and child to wear affect them very much, so let them lie in the pale spiritual colours when they are babies, to feel those loving attributes of the rays, especially of the rose pink and the pale blues.

The pink ray is a feminine ray and that is why we say pink for a girl and blue for a boy. The blue ray is a masculine ray. Pink is derived when white is added to the red ray and is linked to the earth — the blue ray is known as the heavenly blue ray and is associated with the higher worlds. You can introduce the stronger colours after they are a year old but if you have a baby who is more passive, do not hurry their progress and leave them in the paler colours a little longer. I am aware that children are growing up faster today than in the past, but some of this is due to all the stimulus they receive today. We need to keep the child of wonder quality as long as possible — unfortunately the majority of us lose it all too quickly.

Those in companies who are responsible for introducing the colours to be worn by their staff need to think of the effect it will have. When you dress your staff in navy blue they will become impersonal, although more efficient, so make sure you have another warm colour to go with it, for it will help them and the public — they will seem more approachable. When you visit a place and see lovely colours you feel better; quality and output are all affected. I also do not advise grey as a colour to be used as this builds up negativity in the staff. I heard recently of a firm in Europe that had put the staff in grey and found that their turnover went down.

A time will come when staff will be consulted and a vote taken on what colours they would like to wear, for they are the ones who have to wear it. Recently I visited a hairdressing salon where they were proposing to put their staff in black — all they need is for their clients to come in feeling down and depressed and they will think twice before they visit them again, for a person in this instance comes to feel and look better but the black colour will soon make them feel low spirited, even if they are not aware of what is doing it. The colours we see affect us immediately.

I have listed what colours you need for certain health conditions and ways of using those colours. If you work with autistic people you could occasionally wear some orange in your clothing for they would react to it at once. There are so many ways of introducing the colours into our life — it isn't just what you wear, but surroundings are important. Whether in the home or at work, encourage those in your office, factory, shop, and on ships and aeroplanes to think about the colours they use. The power of the colour rays can transform our lives, change our health patterns, our moods, our reactions. On the colour sheet you will find the Colour Wheel. Using your pendulum, ask what colour you need at the present time — it will oscillate between two colours. Taking one of the colours and using the Diagnostic Colour Charts* find out whether you need a tint or a shade of that colour, and then try it with the other colour. You may find you only need one of the colours, or you may need both. The pendulum will say yes or no as you place it over the actual tint or shade.

* The colour turquoise is included in the Diagnostic Colour Charts instead of indigo.

You can also find your colours of activity, rest and inspiration by using the pendulum as I have suggested. This information can be very helpful, for your colour of rest could be either green, blue or violet, and when you wish to be, say, inspired you could find the colour and use it for it could open up new avenues for you to look at and use.

We can use the pendulum this way to find out the right colours for others (always ask for their highest good) and we can then send it to them in absent healing, or tell them that a certain colour will help them and why. When we get the mind to co-operate, and it can be seen to make sense, that colour will become very meaningful for them, and you will learn more about the different colours as you go along. For us to grow spiritually we need all the colours, so it's up to us to tune into their vibration and work with their positive attributes, and our lives will become full of colour, vibrant and fulfilling.

DIET AND COLOUR

Today, interest in nutrition has increased and we have only to read the labels to know what ingredients are in foods. We should avoid artificial colourings and preservatives as much as possible, and eat only natural foods, preferably organically grown produce if possible — as the demand for vegetables grown this way increases, they will become more readily available. Chemicals and artificial fertilizers that are being used today are causing an imbalance within all nature and within us. Fresh fruits and vegetables are all good for us and contain a lot of health giving energy.

There are many good books on the market that give special diets for various complaints and diseases, for instance arthritis patients should not eat meat in any form (those people who have followed this advice and eaten fresh vegetables and fruits etc have found a marked improvement in their health) but let us also be aware when we prepare a meal of the colour content, for the colour of the food is also important.

At the Bristol Cancer Help Centre in Bristol, England, they recommend as part of their diet fresh carrot juice and a lot of green salads. The colour of carrots, as we know, is orange and this feeds us with the orange ray, the colour that recharges the system, gives us energy and vitality, and in this case the will to live and find the energy to keep going. The colour green, in the salads, is the balance within nature and also complements the orange ray. The whole being needs to be uplifted, given a new start and green is always associated with new beginnings.

The bodily system has lost the divine imprint and the green ray will introduce a balance and bring harmony to the body. Any disease is disharmony in the body and can be helped by eating the coloured foods that are suggested for that disease (see the therapeutic uses in The Many Ways of Using Colour for Healing).

A complaint such as anaemia suggests you need the red ray and should therefore eat red foods, for there is a lack of iron in the bloodstream. When the red ray is introduced into the system it forms ions. These are minute particles that carry electro-magnetic energy in the physical body and affect the ferrous cell salt crystals, splitting them into iron and salt. The iron is absorbed and the salt is released through excretion. Red foods also help with mucus and sinus troubles, which can often mean one is having too much dairy produce and that it is clogging up the system. When we have ridges on the nails, this also indicates a clogged up system and orange foods such as oranges, peaches, apricots etc would be ideal to eat. Oranges are particularly rich in vitamin C and were the life-saver during and just after the war for many who had starved and were undernourished. The orange ray also builds up the immune system which is rapidly breaking down today as we live in such a polluted world, for everything we eat affects us, and most of the air we breathe is impure. A hundreds years ago this was not the case but we were not pumping out car fumes and chemical wastes both into the rivers and seas and the atmosphere as we are doing today. Royal Jelly from bees can help to build up the immune system, giving one energy and revitalizing the body generally — it has the colour of the orange ray.

We all need a certain amount of the red and orange ray within us, for apart from the energy content that it gives us, it affects the blood, keeps us earthed and recharges our magnetic energies, which is most important. When our magnetic fields are low we can catch colds and other infections — when we are fit and well, our immune system fights off any invaders. And we all know that when we are unwell we get one thing after another, it takes time to pick ourselves up, because our auras are not radiating out energy, and therefore are not throwing off germs, but absorbing them instead. This is why we then need a tonic or certain medications to help us to recover.

Many who are really fit and well live off uncooked foods in the main, consisting of vegetables, fruits and grains for they are then not killing off the life force energy within the food. They have a lot of energy and their minds are clear, these people also tend to live in the country, so they are not breathing in so much of the polluted atmosphere. In certain parts of the world some people are known to live to well over 100 years old but they mainly live off the land, and in mountainous areas where the air is cleaner.

Where we live is most important to our health and whenever possible we should get out of the towns. Those who live on clay soil find their energy is very earthed as the gravity pull is greater for them than for those who live on sandy soil. They will have to strive harder for anything they wish to accomplish but it is the lesson of perseverance and determination to succeed which comes forward from these individuals. Those people who live on sandy soils will need to earth themselves as their energy will be lighter and freer.

It has been noted that certain environments are more prone to certain diseases but there can be many reasons for this. Foods grown in different environments also have their effect upon us and we should eat the food that is grown in the area where we live. Today we import so much food from different parts of the world and although delicious, in some instances it is affecting our subtle bodies as it links us to the energy from where it came from and those who have handled it. We have all noticed at some time when we go on holiday how the water can upset us and we can become constipated — when this happens add lemon juice to some water and drink it as this helps to clear the toxins from the system, a wonderful cleanser linking to the yellow ray.

Foods in schools and hospitals need to be reviewed, and I'm glad to hear that more schools are becoming aware of the importance of eating good fresh food, for what we eat when we are children will later affect us as adults. But it is just as important to be conscious of the colour of the foods you introduce and to mix them. The same sort of food every day and with no appreciable colour content is enough to put off a child who is not really interested in food, so bring in some different coloured foods. For instance, with a salad there are not only carrots but also red cabbage which would make it look more colourful.

Patients in hospitals do not get better because of the food but in spite of it. Thank goodness for the caring and medical treatment that starts the healing process going. All hospitals need a nutritionist for advice, for example, to eat heavy food after a major operation can be no good for the system. We need light foods and, may I suggest, to be aware of the colour content as this will also help patients to feel better. Only when we ask or demand different standards will we receive them and while we accept food which is either not good for us or has no nutritional value, and grumble behind the scenes, nothing will be done about it.

When we eat fruits like blueberries and bilberries let us be aware that we are absorbing the blue or indigo ray. These are healing rays and have a faster vibration which cleanses and purifies the system. Too much of any given fruit can cause diarrhoea so we need to be wise as to how much we eat at any given time. Black and green grapes are full of sunlight, for the vines only produce the fruit when there is a lot of warm sunny weather, so next time you eat a grape realize you are eating pure sunshine and absorbing the sun's rays.

So many people remove the skins on food as sometimes they can be indigestible, but remember, often the skin is most beneficial for us as it has absorbed more of the light rays. This applies to all foods that are grown above ground; foods that are grown in the ground absorb the earth's energies and we need a balance of both of these energies.

When the nervous system is affected, foods of the yellow ray can be most beneficial. Evening Primrose is often recommended for multiple sclerosis patients and this is linked with the yellow ray, but most general nervous complaints would receive benefit from the yellow ray. Do not use this ray for those who are heading towards a mental nervous breakdown as it will only aggravate their condition. They need a lot of the green ray, so green vegetables would be good for them, and so would carrots and other foods of the orange ray.

We need to get back to our natural rhythms, the rhythms which today have been lost, for we are part of nature and the cycles of the seasons are important for us to tune into. We should eat the foods that are appropriate for that season, make the most of the fruits that are plentiful in the summer months and, when cooking food do not over-cook it, for you lose all the goodness from the vegetables that way. It goes into the water and usually gets poured down the sink. Let us use the colours consciously next time we prepare food, then the cosmic rays will feed us literally.

I have compiled a list of foods by colour so you can see them at a glance — and you may be able to add to the list. The indigo ray comes under the blue ray and it is interesting to note that foods under the red ray and violet ray are at times similar.

——— FOODS AND COLOUR ———

The red ray
Beetroot tops and roots; radishes; aubergine; red-skinned apples; all red-skinned fruits; blackberries; blackcurrants; red peppers.

The orange ray
Oranges and orange juice; mangoes, cantaloupe melons; peaches; apricots; swede; carrots.

The yellow ray

Yellow peppers; grapefruit; golden corn; yams; honeydew melons; bananas; marrow; pineapples; lemons.

The green ray

All green vegetables.

The blue ray

Plums; blueberries; bilberries.

The violet ray

Aubergines; purple broccoli; beetroot tops; purple grapes; blackberries.

NUMEROLOGY
AND COLOUR

Your name and birthdate when linked to the numbers and colours reveal your inner self, your inner potential, and will show you whether you are using your abilities, how you react towards other people, whether you are assertive or hold back and in what areas you can use your abilities, if you are not already doing so. Numbers have always carried power and nothing in our universe is chance, all is harmony at one level. It is a question of understanding the keys that open the doorway, and our interpretation, that help us to become aware of deeper knowledge.

Most people take for granted that seven days make one week, about four weeks make a month and 12 months add up to one year but all of this is part of an ordered universe. With numbers we are again dealing with vibrations, and the vibratory number for the earth is seven. Let us remind ourselves that there are also seven musical notes, the seven seas, seven major planets and all ancient teachings talk about the seven chakras within man. It is also known that all the cells in the body are renewed every seven years. But we can look at seven in another way, for within the number seven is the symbol of the heavenly worlds and the earth. Take a triangle that has three equal sides, with its sides resting on each other: there is no stress, the points are equally distant from each other and it is the symbolic representation of God. Within the triangle there are four more equilateral triangles (see diagram). This new number, four, represents the earth and when we add the three from the triangle and the four from the further triangles within it, we have a total of seven. Everything is linked to a number in the same way that everything is made up of colour. Hidden within the triangle are the four further triangles which also are in harmony with each other. But if we make a square shape, using the number four, (see diagram) we get four corners. On earth, we are represented by the square but have within us the divine harmony of the triangle. Great teachings throughout time have told us of this key — we all tend to look outwards for our happiness and peace but it lies within ourselves, and that is why it has long been said 'Man Know Thyself'. God is within, harmony is within, but we have to change ourselves by working on ourselves, lifting our vibrations. We can do this through colour and seeing ourselves in the light.

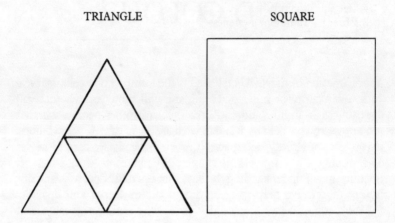

TRIANGLE   SQUARE

KEY TO THE NUMBERS
___ AND THEIR VIBRATIONS ___

1 Leadership, independence.
2 Adaptability, can hold back, leads one to harmony.
3 The pure artist.
4 Practicality, self-discipline.
5 Communication, a tendency to go down too many avenues.
6 Responsibility, the organizer.
7 Sensitivity, insight.
8 Balancing of spirit and matter, material affairs, business acumen, success.
9 Service, benevolence, giving of oneself with no thought of reward.

KEY TO THE COLOURS AND THEIR VIBRATIONS

1 Red	Willpower, determination to succeed.	
2 Orange	Creativity, self-expression, leading to confidence.	
3 Yellow	Intellect, ideas.	
4 Green	Energy, balance and harmony.	
5 Blue	Intuition, awareness.	
6 Indigo	Power with knowledge and understanding.	
7 Violet	High ideals, inspiration, intuition.	
8 Silver	Unifying knowledge with awareness.	
9 Golden yellow	Serving for the sake of serving, to give without thought of self.	

The following are examples of how you can use this information. Take your birthdate and add up the numbers as in the example below. This will give an overall number and that is the vibration you are working with. The other numbers have also some importance as you will see. The odd numbers are the masculine principle and the even numbers are the feminine principle.

NUMBER ONE VIBRATION – THE RED RAY

Number one is leadership, those who have initiative and are not afraid of using it. They are independent, often forward thinkers and can be pioneers in their field. They accept responsibility and are always active in one way or another.

This is a strong masculine energy linking to the Father principle, and without the feminine principle working within this person they can become bombastic and overbearing. They can have a feeling of self-importance and like to be noticed. When the number one comes forward in the birthdate, even when not the final number, that person has within them leadership. It may not have shown itself so far, but once you are aware you have it within, use it, activate that energy within yourself, link into the red ray to give you the energy you need. Sometimes as a child you may have been suppressed and not allowed to use your abilities

— this knowledge helps us to uncover our true selves, and then we can go forward and use the energy.

Example

BIRTHDATE: 4 March 1947

4. 3. 1947

We add the numbers together and bring them down to a single digit.

$4+3 + (1+9) + (4+7)$
$4+3 + (1+0) + (1+1)$
$4+3+1+2$
$4+3+3 = 10 = 1$

Here is a person who has a number one vibration and is therefore a leader, certainly not backward in coming forward, and can use their energy in many constructive ways. The one vibration is linked to the red ray, so here we would find a person with a lot of energy, and if it is not channelled into something positive it can become destructive. These people need a job to fulfil them otherwise they can become so frustrated that they get up to mischief — there is a lot of potential here that can be used in many ways.

The number four here would indicate a person who is practical and into self-discipline, the three vibration is someone who has a lot of creativity within them and they must express it, otherwise they will become very frustrated. Think of the peach colour within the orange ray to bring out one's creativity.

When we add the day of our birthday and the month to the current year, this gives us our year number. You can work these out for each year but, taking an example of 1988, as this is the year of writing, I will show you how it works. The year 1988 adds up to an eight, the number of balance and awareness and would have brought many changes. When we take the birth day above, and the month, and add it to 1988 we have:

4. 3. 1988
$4+3+1+16$
$1+5 = 6$

The number six is to take responsibility for all one's actions. The eight being the year of balance, we wish to clear the dross of many past issues. 'Forgive and let go' is a good saying here, and many changes and new directions would have come forward for you which will bear fruit. You can now work out the number for you at the time of reading.

NUMBER TWO VIBRATION — THE ORANGE RAY

Adaptability leading to harmony, this vibration is duality, and we live in a world of duality, day and night, positive and negative, male and female etc. Number two is the opposite of number one, who is very definite. These people are adaptable, and they avoid conflicts but have strong moods and feelings. They can be very lovable, and enjoy working with others, but never take them for granted or they will not forgive you. They love their home, and need a home as a base — should they lose their home they could become disorientated. Once they find something that interests them they pursue it to the extreme and can become good at it. They are not intellectuals but can become scholars. They are perfectly happy to work for someone else but do need a lot of support at times in their life.

The two vibration is the orange ray of expression and they need to use their talents by creating a lovely environment for everyone to enjoy. They need to make things and express their creativity otherwise they will become very frustrated. There is a tendency to hold back, but they should stand up for their rights for they have much to give inwardly and know it.

Example

BIRTHDATE: 21 February 1941
           21. 2. 1941
           3+2+1+5
           3+2+6 = 11 = 2

When you have two as the number or part of the number for your birthday, you are a person who can hold back and here, with two as the second month, the same applies. A person with so many twos is likely to be shy and need encouragement in all they do. Within them they have a lot of creativity linking to the number three, being the pure artist, and with good ideas the number five with the one could take the initiative. A person who loves their home but still needs to find a greater purpose to find their fulfillment. When we take the birthdate and, as an example, add the year 1988 we have:

    21. 2. 1988
    3+2+1+16
    3+2+8 = 13 = 4

The number four is practicality and self-discipline, which would mean not an easy year for you, but it would have been a time to clear up your affairs and to make a fresh start, find a new project and have new interests.

NUMBER THREE VIBRATION — THE YELLOW RAY

Creativity: here we have the pure artist. To create is one of the highest expressions a person can achieve on earth, and we can create at many levels: children, works of art, beautiful surroundings but what we create we have to live with and this needs to be remembered by the number three vibration. For these people, life is to be enjoyed. They tend to give quite a lot of themselves in time and energy, but they need to be wanted and loved. They usually have lots of acquaintances, and they like to be involved in many interesting things.

The three vibration knows within that life is or should be creative and more fun than the majority of people make it out to be and these people have the capacity to bring others to life. This is the yellow ray of ideas and knowledge and this can be given out in many ways.

Example

BIRTHDATE: 7 May 1971
        7+5+1+8
        7+5+9 = 21 = 3

The number three vibration, with all their creativity, would certainly have many ideas through the number five vibration if this featured in the birthdate. The seven is sensitivity and to be a true artist you need this sensitivity. A person with these numbers could be a good artist, and give pleasure to many through their creative art, whether as a painter, sculptor, designer or whatever. The three vibration could also be the scientist, bringing forth new ideas for mankind through their sensitivity — there are many ways of expression once one is tuned into the ray of knowledge and ideas. The nine vibration here would give them a longing to serve and help others in some way, to find an outlet for this energy otherwise this person would be unhappy. When, as an example, we add the birthdate to the year 1988 we have:

7. 5. 1988
7+5+1+16
7+5+8 = 20 = 2

A year when you would have needed a push to accomplish what was to be done. The two vibration encourages one to be more adaptable and this leads to harmony. With the sensitivity of the number seven and the five vibration of ideas, there would be a tendency to go inwards, to review your life, before going forward.

NUMBER FOUR VIBRATION — THE GREEN RAY

The ray of practicality. Ask a four vibration to do anything for you and here we have the willing workhorse. Everything has to have a meaning and purpose for them but they are realistic and objective. They either have a lot of self-discipline or will have incarnated to learn self-discipline: that is the essence of the four vibration.

They can be generous by nature and stingy at the same time — rather a paradox — but this is the green ray of expansion and they give their time to the community in many ways. They make good doctors and nurses, also teachers. Usually they have a lot of stamina and can carry heavy loads on their shoulders, but they tend to worry a lot, even if there is nothing to worry about, and for all that they make good counsellors and therapists. They have an understanding of others' needs and can be compassionate. They have a need to be with people who can activate them as they can become static. This always applies to the green ray, being the middle of the spectrum. Harmony is important to us all but we need movement as well. Four is very much an earth number (we have the four races of mankind, the four seasons, the four elements, we talk about the four corners of the earth and north, south, east, west).

Example

BIRTHDATE: 19 July 1958
19. 7. 1958
10+7+1+13
1+7+5 = 13 = 4

This would be a person who is very practical and having a strong one vibration, which is leadership, would do well at anything they decided to do. The one vibration is the red ray and the four vibration is the green ray: complementary colours that can work very harmoniously together. If they find a focus for their energies they should do very well. The seven vibration is sensitivity — be careful you do not identify with other people's problems, a tendency of the seven vibration. The five vibration means you have many good ideas and you can be very inventive with your sensitivity. At some point in your life you will become very interested in the spiritual philosophies of life and with these numbers you should be able to simplify the knowledge for others to be able to relate to it. An opportunity here for great expansion at many levels.

When we add the birthdate to the year 1988 we have:

19. 7. 1988
10+7+1+16
$1+7+8 = 16 = 7$

A year when you could have accomplished a lot and settled old accounts in many ways. With the seven vibration of sensitivity you would have been aware of what you had to do and the one vibration gave you energy and determination to do it. A time of looking at oneself: 'Where am I going, what is life about?' For those who have not previously been interested, this was the year you started to look for the deeper purpose and meaning of life.

NUMBER FIVE VIBRATION — THE BLUE RAY

The number of communication. These people have to watch they do not go down too many avenues and waste time; they need to find a goal and go for it. The person who is a five vibration has a need to express themselves in many ways, through speaking, writing, singing, communicating in some way, otherwise they can become withdrawn — a negative aspect of the blue ray. These people have strong opinions and tastes, often concerned with health, and they can be critical and unsociable. They are very restless and need space, they often lack energy and can overdo things, so they need to find a balance from within. There is a need to be more flexible; once they have found their path they forge ahead, but they need constant change and many interests to keep them going.

The five links to the five virtues, which are Goodness, Judgement, Love, Wisdom and Truth. We all need to truly understand and incorporate these virtues into our lives. We can work with the colour and the virtue — this way it has a powerful effect — and I have given you the colours and the virtues on page 24. When the person who is a five vibration has a deeper understanding of life, they often become healers, teachers or counsellors, but they need to rededicate themselves each day to keep their focus and not dissipate their energies. Anyone who finds it difficult to concentrate should find something that truly interests them and become fully involved with it. This is a good training for the mind and energies and they will surprise themselves.

Example

BIRTHDATE: 6 November 1977
6. 11. 1977
6+2+1+14
6+2+6 = 14 = 5

The five vibration is a person interested in many things but with the six vibration also figuring here, it is the number of responsibility and the organizer — and with the two sixes are very good at the job. The two vibration means they must be adaptable and heed others' needs, can be shy but when they lose themselves in their work this goes for they become aware of their abilities within. They also make good delegators — the six vibration — and with their many good ideas help others to tap into their potential. The four vibration that comes forward when we add the two sevens together means a person who can be practical at times.

It should be noted that 1977 was an important year for it brought forward a reawakening and longing by many to get into deeper issues and take responsibility for this planet. Over the last 10 years many have become more aware of environmental issues, how polluted the atmosphere has become and the importance of our health. It is up to us to do something about it. The year 1988 was the year of greater awareness of deep issues and made us more aware that we have to take responsibility for our actions for we live with the result of those actions, which are having a deep effect upon the earth. It is interesting therefore to see that 1977 is (1+4) = six, the number of responsibility, and the year 1988 is (1+16) = eight, the number of balance and awareness.

When we link the birthdate to the year 1988 we have:

6. 11. 1988
6+2+1+16
6+2+8 = 16 = 7

For this person, 1988 would have been a year of great awareness and of looking within for many changes which would help them grow spiritually. The seven links to the violet ray of higher aspiration and inspiration helping them to understand the changes that came about.

NUMBER SIX VIBRATION — ——— THE INDIGO RAY ———

This is the number of responsibility. These people must watch they do not take on too much. Efficient and very capable, whatever they undertake it will be done well. They can organize and delegate and are good at running events of any kind. They are home lovers, their home is their sanctuary and should they lose their home they can become disorientated. They are very caring and could be good therapists in any field or run a clinic, or an office. They need to be with people for balance as they tend to be loners.

They are very faithful and can keep a promise, they are amazingly loyal and devoted, and even when they feel let down they have a strong forgiving streak. These people really need a partner, for they can be lonely and sad; they put all their energies into what they are doing, quite often to counteract the loneliness they feel and do not accept. When they meet the right person they come to life. They have a deep understanding of others' needs.

A testing vibration and one which demands that they follow through with any endeavour. One cannot always see the outcome but as long as the motives are good they should go forward knowing all is well.

Example

BIRTHDATE: 13 January 1963
          13. 1. 1963
          4+1+1+9
          4+1+10
          4+1+1 = 6

The six vibration is responsibility. The number 13 has the one of leadership and the three of creativity and, as it makes four, this person must use their abilities in a practical way. The two ones here indicate a person who can initiate anything, pioneer a new project and see it through, but it would have to be something everyone could relate to for it to do well. If ever these people found themselves with no money they would soon assert themselves and find ways of using their abilities to keep going, for the one vibration is the red ray, the vibration of courage and determination to succeed.

When we link the birthdate to the year 1988 we have:

13. 1. 1988
4+1+1+16
4+1+8 = 13 = 4

The year of 1988 was when you came into a greater awareness of life, you looked more deeply into your motives and what you wanted to do with your life. The four vibration, being half of the eight vibration, acts as a reflection and brings balance and new beginnings and, providing you listened to the intuitive side of yourself, only good could come from any endeavour started in the year of 1988. There should have been changes in your life, which will reap their just reward.

NUMBER SEVEN VIBRATION — THE VIOLET RAY

Sensitivity and insight. This vibration is associated with extra-sensory perception, an awareness of other dimensions. Many are mediums with this number; they can also be the practical mystic, earthing the knowledge they receive to enable others to understand. These people are often not very earthed, and to many have their heads in the clouds, highly sensitive to everything. They have to learn the lesson of loving detachment, for they are easily hurt, and they can have deep emotional problems. Often they try to stop others from making mistakes but then come to realize that we only learn through our mistakes and we therefore have to stand aside sometimes.

Very philosophical people, they make lovely companions for they have lively minds and many interests but they must watch their health as they do not have stamina. They are very friendly, identify with other people's problems and can take on their conditions. They give unstintingly and often unwisely, need rest and do not like too much routine.

Example

BIRTHDATE: 27 March 1939
          27. 3. 1939
          9+3+1+12
          9+3+4 = 16 = 7

The two vibration linked with the seven vibration will mean this life is not easy, but the person will learn through life's experiences how to overcome their lack of confidence, for whenever we have a two in front of a number there is a tendency to hold back and withdraw. With the three vibration, they will have a lot of creative ideas which they will express in many ways, trying to bring some joy into people's lives. With the seven vibration they will be very sensitive and will feel drawn to anything religious. As children they were aware of another world or reality, and they may have developed their abilities in the direction where they can share their understanding of other realities.

Twenty-seven makes a nine, the vibration of the server and the four vibration will help them to be practical, as there is a tendency with the seven vibration to overwork. When we link the birthdate to the year 1988 we have:

   27. 3. 1988
   9+3+1+16
   9+3+8 =20 = 2

This would have been a year of adaptability but with it a greater awareness of life's purpose. A year to look at your material affairs and take stock, and to see where you are going in your life. Success came to you but not quite the way you expected.

NUMBER EIGHT VIBRATION — THE SILVER RAY

The eight vibration is the balance of spirit and matter, the eight being formed by two circles, one on top of the other ('As above, so below'). Above are the heavenly worlds and below is the earth — here are the two principles working together: spirit and matter, the masculine and feminine, which are within each and every one of us. We are spiritual beings living and working in matter.

This number's vibration is power and success but it is what we do with this energy that is important. When it is to help others, spiritual power will move in to help us; when it is for personal gain we are successful for a while and then lose what we think we have gained, for we have not learned the lesson of allowing the money to flow in and out. Eight is also a business number and can indicate a materialist but when spiritually orientated the goal is to bring heaven to earth, whether through knowledge or to beautify the surroundings. We have to have the right intentions and motives and never lose sight of our goal.

When we truly understand the right use of power then we shall have learnt a big lesson, for true power is non-power and success is only fleeting when compared to our main goal: to share that which we have and bring joy, hope, peace and love to our brothers and sisters as we journey through time on earth.

Example

BIRTHDATE: 14 June 1950
14. 6. 1950
5+6+1+5
5+6+6 = 17 = 8

The five vibration here indicates a person who is active and into many ventures. They feel very responsible for all they undertake — this is the six vibration. Only the best of everything here will do, there is a need to watch their health as they could overwork and become a workaholic. They must remember relationships are important and nourish them, for here I see the classic example of some of our top businessmen and women who make their goal business success and that is all that matters, only to find they are very lonely inside. We must always balance our two natures within and not forget the feminine aspect — this applies whether you are a man or woman. To be successful gives one a feeling of satisfaction but we are multi-faceted beings and we need to nourish every level of our being.

When we add the birthdate to the year 1988 we have:

14. 6. 1988
5+6+1+16
5+6+8 = 19 = 1

This year would have been important for you, perhaps a new beginning in your life or a new venture. The one vibration would have given you the impetus to start something new; at the same time the nine vibration would have given you a longing to find a deeper purpose to your life and to review your motives and actions.

NUMBER NINE VIBRATION — THE GOLDEN YELLOW RAY

This is the number of service. To serve for the sake of serving with no thought of any reward is the highest vibration that mankind can tune in to, and so often the reward comes anyway. We should not look for results of what we are doing, just to give of our time and energy in whatever way the spirit moves us is enough. All this is so contrary to the materialist of today who is always looking for profit, but there is a time and place for us all to arrive at these points in life and we should allow others their space to experience life the way they wish to.

The so-called saints are often misunderstood, yet revered when they are dead, and a person with this vibration, and in tune with it, has high ideals and wishes to help alleviate other people's suffering. They like to share their knowledge and experience to help mankind grow and at the same time understand the meaning and purpose of life. They do not have to be known and often work behind the scenes but accomplish a lot — benevolent, kind, loving, giving and sharing what they have.

This is the path we shall all tread eventually but only after many lifetimes. It is up to us in each incarnation to earn a little more spiritual gold in our auras until, like some of the saints, our very presence becomes a blessing to others and we do not have to have the nine vibration to have these qualities.

Example

BIRTHDATE: 17 March 1960
          17. 3. 1960
          8+3+1+6
          8+3+7 = 18 = 9

With the one and the seven as the birthday it would be a difficult incarnation. The one is leadership and the seven vibration is sensitivity — people who are sensitive are often shy and yet they need to take the lead in many ways, and to balance these two energies. They would have had many experiences when they were young and in overcoming these are in a position to help others in life. The eight is the number of balance:

using energies that enhance each other and work together.

The nine is a very benevolent number, and these people are only happy when helping or doing something for others. They do not ask for any reward and just get on with life. The number nine links to the golden yellow, the ray of wisdom and knowledge and, with the numbers one and seven and eight, they should accomplish many things, mainly helping humanity and in some way leaving their mark. When we add the birthdate to the year 1988 we have:

17. 3. 1988
8+3+1+16
8+3+8 = 19 = 1

This year would have been very important, a time to review the past, and would have brought many changes: a time to let go of what has gone before to make way for the future. Using their resources in many ways, perhaps helping those less fortunate, but in whatever way their presence has been felt — it was a turning point in their lives.

The birthdates chosen were just examples of how to use numerology with colour. The year 1988, which adds up to an eight was an important year for everyone: a time of change, a time to reassess one's life and look at one's motivation, clear the dross and link with the highest within ourselves. And let us recall that the eight is showing us the two circles of spirit and matter — we should work with matter but not to get so involved with matter that we forget we are spiritual beings. Having seen these worked examples, you should be able to do your own readings for your date of birth and for any other year you choose.

The name we are given at birth is also very important for it holds a vibration that is just for you. Yes, there are many names the same but the surnames differ, as do the middle names, and the alphabet is again linked to the colour rays. When we shorten or abbreviate a name we change the energy, so we need to remember this when we allow others to call us any name they choose. Some people go so far as to change their names by deed poll when they are adults as they take some exception to the name that was given to them at birth.

If you choose a name for a baby, remember the importance of the name and how it will affect that person, for they will probably have it for life. The name we give our home or business does more for it than perhaps many realize — check it on the chart below and see what vibrations are surrounding your home or office every time you mention it by name. The right name with the right vibrations can change any situation, but it has to be a vibration you are in tune with then it will work *for* you, not *against* you.

Every time our names are spoken we are receiving colour light rays which are feeding our auric field. When a woman marries she takes on the surname of the man she marries and the energy around her changes, but it's only noticeable after a period of time. Today some women keep their own surname and add their husband's name on at the end — these are choices we can all make.

Using the seven colours of the rainbow and linking them to the alphabet, we can find out what colours we have in our name and how are they affecting us, for they indicate abilities we have and our attitudes to life. You will need to refer to the numbers and their vibrations and colours and their vibrations. Colour is also linked to sound: the key of A is indigo, the key of B is violet, the key of C is red, and so on. Bearing this in mind, we can then link the colours to the alphabet in the following way:

Indigo	Violet	Red	Orange	Yellow	Green	Blue
A	B	C	D	E	F	G
H	I	J	K	L	M	N
O	P	Q	R	S	T	U
V	W	X	Y	Z	—	—

Now we can take a name and link it to the colours, for example, Winston Churchill was known throughout the world and is famous still. A man of many facets, he was a Member of Parliament for over 50 years and became Prime Minister during the last war and 1951-55. His inspiration during the last war will always be remembered. An artist and author, he exhibited at the Royal Academy in London and was awarded the Nobel Prize for Literature in 1953. A man of action who lived life to the full.

Use all the names to get a full reading, for this is the complete energy a person is born with:

Name: W I N S T O N   L E O N A R D
Colour: V V B Y G I B   Y Y I B I O O
Name: S P E N C E R   C H U R C H I L L
Colour: Y V Y B R Y O   R I B O R I V Y Y

To arrive at the above you take the letter W and find its colour on the chart, which is then placed below it, then the next letter and so on until we have all the colours of the name. We then add up the colours to see how many of the red ray we have etc. We also need to know how many vowels and consonants there are in the name, and subtract one from the other. The vowels are feminine, our intuitive aspect within us, while the consonants are masculine; so within a name we have both masculine and feminine.

Vowels:	A	E	I	O	U
Colours:	I	Y	V	I	B
How many:	1	3	2	2	1

Although in the chart I started with indigo, the chart below starts with the red ray simply to make it easier to read off the colours.

Colour	Total	Vowels	Consonants
Red	3	—	3
Orange	4	—	4
Yellow	8	3	5
Green	1	—	1
Blue	5	1	4
Indigo	5	3	2
Violet	4	2	2

The above now shows us how many we have of each colour. The colours of the vowels are subtracted from the totals for each colour in the name to arrive at the number of consonants. The consonants show our outer expression whereas the vowels are our intuitive feelings.

THE READING

The three of red shows the strong leadership he portrayed with a good mind to carry out anything he 'set his mind' to. The four of orange indicates his creative expression and, as he had four here, whatever he did would be with a strong practical approach. Although it has been said that at school he didn't do very well, with eight of yellow he could have been bored and only did well when he was really interested in the subject, for here is a man with a good intellect who had many ideas. With the five of indigo he had power with knowledge and knew how to communicate when it was necessary, linking into the fives of both blue and indigo.

He loved painting and with the four of orange and four of violet he was very creative, practical and self-disciplined. A very sensitive man, with the twos of indigo and violet, but he would rarely show it. The two would indicate that he could hold back from showing his deepest feelings even to those who were very close to him. The blue ray is interesting as he has five — very intuitive and aware, he certainly did go down many avenues in his life, and had an awareness of his destiny and knew that while the war was on no harm would come to him as he had a purpose to fulfil.

Deep down inside he loved peace — this is the green ray with the one vibration — and it was certainly important to him. He had a lot of energy and unless he was active mentally or doing something worthwhile he was very restless. The yellow ray seems to dominate the reading, with the eight of yellow, and with his many experiences he would be drawing on the golden yellow of wisdom to discover how to express himself with all the ideas he had, but he was aware of his power and knew it needed to be used wisely. He was a man of his time, much needed and loved.

Another name well known to history is Florence Nightingale. Here is dedication and determination and she has the following colours:

Name: F L O R E N C E   N I G H T I N G A L E
Colour: G Y I O Y B R Y   B V B I G V B B I Y Y

Vowels:	A	E	I	O	U
Colours:	I	Y	V	I	B
How many:	1	3	2	1	

Colour	Total	Vowels	Consonants
Red	1	—	1
Orange	1	—	1
Yellow	5	3	2
Green	2	—	2
Blue	5	—	5
Indigo	3	2	1
Violet	2	2	—

THE READING

The one of the red ray shows determination to succeed at all costs and that she could be very independent. That she could be very expressive when she wanted to be is shown by the orange ray; with the five of yellow she had good ideas and with the feminine aspect of the three she knew intuitively she had a job to do. The blue ray of five shows awareness of what was needed at the time, and she used her ability to communicate to make known in the right quarter what she required. As we know she had a very difficult time but with the one vibration of red and orange she would have been a very determined lady.

The violet ray shows high ideals and sensitivity to others' needs, and she used her intuiton through the indigo and blue rays to bring healing and help to those in need. The two of yellow in the consonants would mean she had to inspire others about her work so that they could help her. Even though she has the one vibration of the red and orange ray, the two vibration of the yellow could have held her back.

What I have given here is an overview of two very famous people, very different in every way, but who left their mark on all of us.

Sometimes just changing your name slightly can help to change the energy, as with the names Charlie and Charles. When you check it against the chart you will see that Charlie, which sounds softer anyway as a vibration, has a violet that the name of Charles does not have — instead we have another yellow in the name of Charles:

Name: C H A R L I E   C H A R L E S
Colour: R I I O Y V Y   R I I O Y Y Y

The different vibration will eventually have an effect. You can also take the names of Richard and Dick, for example:

Name: R I C H A R D   D I C K
Colour: O V R I I O O   O V R O

The difference here lies in the indigo ray which links us to deeper issues in our lives. When red, yellow or blue are missing from your name, attract the colours to you using the methods described above as it indicates that you need them.

MEDITATIONS
WITH COLOUR

THE SEVEN RAYS

We can start the day by tuning into the seven rays — the rainbow colours we see through a prism.

Sit comfortably and take some deep breaths. As you breathe out, feel yourself relax more and more. Imagine a golden ball of light above your head, see or feel this light pour into you filling every part of your being. As it does it disperses all tension, stress and negativity. Breathe in the red ray up through the soles of your feet to the solar plexus and feel it pour into every part of you, into every cell, organ and tissue. This ray will energize you, cleanse the blood and give you a feeling of warmth. Just breathe naturally in and out and feel yourself relax more and more as the warmth pervades your being. Finally, breathe out the red ray. (Do not use the red ray if you have had any heart trouble — think of the pink ray relaxing you and warming you instead.)

Breathe in the orange ray up through the soles of the feet to the solar plexus and feel it permeate every part of you, feel a sense of joy enter your being for this is a new day, a new beginning. The orange ray will give you vitality, confidence and the ability to be yourself. Release the past, let go, let God's love and wisdom pour into you through this orange ray and you know all is well. Breathe out the orange ray.

Breathe in the yellow ray, up through the soles of the feet, feel the golden yellow ray fill your being, bringing you a feeling of well-being. This ray brings new ideas and links us to divine wisdom. Ask for divine wisdom in all your affairs. This ray will relax the solar plexus and release pent up emotions and stress — breathe these out and feel a lightness enter your being. The yellow ray tunes us into divine mind — this is the ray that illuminates our minds and gives us luminous thoughts. Feel the golden yellow radiate in and through you. Breathe out the yellow ray.

The green ray now enters your being, horizontally. Breathe in a beautiful light green — this colour affects the heart centre and brings peace and harmony to your whole being. Feel your heart centre relax, all the tension in this area is released; also think of the pink ray of love and feel this pour into your being. Love yourself and send forth love to all those you care for — this is the ray of brotherhood and fellowship and as we bless others, so we are blessed. Breathe out the green ray.

Now breathe in the blue ray. This is the blue you see on a summer's day — feel it enter through the crown at the top of the head and pour into you, as though you were an empty vessel, filling you up with this healing ray to the tips of your fingers to the tips of your toes. The blue ray renews our faith and trust and gives us a knowledge that all is well. Allow your soul to express itself through you, for we all have a purpose for being here, and on each breath relax more and more. For any area you feel is tense, breathe in the blue ray to that area and then relax. Breathe out the blue ray.

Breathe in the indigo ray, the ray of knowledge with power. This is the colour of midnight blue. Imagine it pouring into you through the crown centre and then into the solar plexus, filling your whole being with this colour. This ray will purge you of dross — ask that you receive this ray to the extent it is right for you and for your highest good. Ask for knowledge and understanding to help you with your life and know that as you ask you receive. Breathe out the indigo ray.

And so to the beautiful violet ray. Breathe in the violet colour through your crown centre, see it or imagine it pouring into your solar plexus and then filling your whole being. This ray links us to all that is beautiful and true. Let go of your lower desires and raise your thoughts to receive a high ideal. Let us ask that we can be of service to others, for as we give to another we receive. Imagine a chalice pouring out love, healing and blessings. We are that chalice and as it is emptied we know it will be refilled with that which we pour forth. Breath out the violet ray.

We can finish by saying: 'May I always be aware that I live, move and have my being within God's divine cosmic rays.' Make sure you close yourself after any meditation: see yourself in a cloak of light and ask the light to protect you, bless you and guide you for your highest good.

———— A VISIT TO THE SUN ————

Relax and breathe deeply, ask the light to protect you as you meditate, and see or feel this light enfold and surround you. Close your eyes and focus your attention on your brow centre and see yourself sitting on a beach: the sand is golden and soft to the touch, the sea is lapping on the shore, you are alone and as you look up the sun is just coming up over the horizon. Feel the sun's rays pour over you, bringing you life and warmth.

There is not a cloud in the sky and the trees are still. This is the beginning of a new day, a fresh start, and as you sit there watch the sun as it rises higher and higher in the sky. As it does so it spreads its rays onto the water and these form a ladder reaching upward into the sky. Get up and walk towards the ladder, put your feet on the first step and start to climb up into the sun. The sun is warmer now and you feel so relaxed. Gradually, as you get nearer to the sun, the rays penetrate your whole being, your soul becomes alive and you feel a wholeness you have never felt before, and then you are inside the sun.

A feeling of oneness with all creation sweeps over you and time stands still; you realize that all your longings of the soul will come true, you feel the sun caress you in its warmth, you are filled with inspiration for here all is known. Breathe in the light, bathe in the rays, as here you become aware of who you truly are and know you are a divine spark of the living God. Ask for energy, for the inspiration you need for your work, for ideas, creativity, and how we can beautify the earth, and pray that God's will will be done through you.

It is now time to leave, so give thanks for all you have received and slowly start to descend the ladder. Once again you are sitting on the seashore, the sun is now high in the sky, there is a slight breeze but it is warm. Be aware as you go through the day of all God's cosmic rays, as you are aware they will help you. Colour is the language of God, so paint yourself whatever colour you require and realize they are living light rays and that you are part of them. Think of others in the light as you go through the day and thank God for all your blessings. See a robe of many colours around you, sense it or feel it and close your chakra centres as though you were closing a flower.

THE PURE
___ WHITE LIGHT OF PEACE ___

Breathe in and relax all tension out through the feet. Imagine yourself in a ball of light and that this light will protect you as you enter the meditation. Close your eyes and feel the crown centre tingle as it fills with light, then send this light to the base chakra. The light strengthens the red ray and brings courage and strength as it pours into you; feel it flowing through you and into the blood. Now picture the light flowing into the solar plexus, filling you with divine order and wisdom — see or imagine the gold light flow out from you and round you. It gives you a sense of joy and upliftment and fills your being with divine ideas.

The light now enters the heart centre and pink flows through this centre. Send forth love from your centre to the world; the gold from the solar plexus mingles with the pink of love and wisdom and it flows through you and then out into the world. Any organ that is unwell fill with love and say 'Love, love, love'.

Send the light to the roof of the mouth. This is the power centre of indigo. Think of faith, strength, wisdom, justice, love and light and then see the brow centre filled with light. This is the centre of imagination. Think of goodness and beauty and truth, let your will go and ask for God's will to be done through you — this will bring joy, peace, fellowship and brotherhood. Centre the light on the stomach area — this is the area of emotion — and see the green ray of divine order enter this area — also a clear orange, see it pulsating and clearing away the dross.

The light now enters the base of the brain, the area of enthusiasm. Feel all the colours pour through you soothing you and giving you all you need for your highest good. Let the healing power of God enter into every part of your being, and then see these colours go out into the cosmos. Ask the white light to enfold and protect you for the highest good.

___ THE WAVES OF THE SEA ___

Imagine the room in a blue light, breathe it out into the atmosphere, filling all the space in the room where you are sitting, and close your eyes. Breathe deeply and relax: relax your face muscles and all your body, become immersed in the white light. This light is cleansing and purifying. Let us imagine the light as waves of the sea.

The sea is lapping over your feet, relaxing and soothing them. Like the tide, very slowly the waves begin to get higher until eventually they are over your knees, then over the legs, hips — you know it is all right for this is the sea of light. As it pours over your solar plexus you relax more and more, up to the heart, purifying all your energies as it rises, then to the throat, until the white light covers all of you. The white waves strengthen you, give you a feeling of upliftment and bring you healing.

Now ask for the blue light of peace, truth, faith, and trust to touch your feet. As waves of the blue light start to cover your whole being, imagine them going into every cell, organ and tissue, filling all your centres within. From the centre of your being, feel this light go to others and see them bathed in the blue light, the healing blue light; see them renewed and uplifted and know that this healing blue ray of God has touched them. Give thanks for what you have received and ask the light to protect you and bless you always.

THE WATER LILY

Breathe deeply and relax, relax on every breath, close your eyes, focus your attention on the brow centre and see in front of you a pond. Growing on the surface are water lillies. The pond is surrounded by several trees and one of them is a weeping willow. Its branches touch the water like a caress, the day is warm and you are dressed in light clothing. Walk towards the pond and look inside the water lily that is nearest to you: the golden stamens shimmer, the petals are smooth and white and they form a cup receiving the sun's rays.

You long to be able to get inside the water lily and suddenly find yourself getting smaller and smaller, so small that you now can step inside and lie down on the golden stamens. As you do so you feel yourself being cleansed and purified, your heart is filled with love, the stamens enfold you and bathe you in the gold light. Very gently the water lily rocks you to and fro on the water and your being begins to tingle with a feeling of wonder and joy. The petals of pure white seem to have a pink glow and this permeates your being, the sun's rays continue to pour down on you and are warming and soothing and relaxing. Think of someone who would benefit from these rays and send the light to them with love for their highest good.

Now become aware of yourself and realize it is time to leave. Step ashore onto the grass and find yourself becoming larger and larger until you are your normal size again. You sense a great white light around you like a cloak — this will protect you as long as you are aware of it. Give thanks for all you have received and, when you are ready, take a deep breath, move your hands and feet and open your eyes.

THE ROSE GARDEN

Relax and breathe deeply, each breath making you relax more and more, and ask the white light to protect you as you enter the silence. Focus your attention on the brow centre and see yourself standing in front of a wooden door. It has several steps leading up to it; walk towards it and open it. You enter a walled rose garden with hundreds of roses of every colour, size and shape. The fragrance is breathtaking, there are many pathways leading to the centre and you decide to walk down one of them, passing very slowly the many coloured roses on either side of you.

As you reach the centre there is a beautiful rosebush with pink roses; some are still only buds and some of them are fully opened. Choose one of the flowers and if it is a bud see it open in your mind's eye. Breathe in the pink from the rose and feel it pour into you, warming, soothing and relaxing you until you feel yourself in a pink cloud from your feet to your head. Breathe in the perfume from the rose and, as you do so, you have a feeling of becoming at one with the rose. You are now radiating the pink light and a beautiful fragrance and you realize why roses are associated with love, the love that gives without any thought of return.

Gradually the rose turns white and a white light surrounds you. Breathe in this white light, feel it enter every part of you, and as you breathe out all that is negative and harmful is dispelled from you. See the light enter the crown of your head; as you breathe in feel as though you are an empty vessel and open yourself to receive the pink light of God's love. Do this for a while, breathing in the light and breathing out all that is negative and harmful, until you feel yourself becoming all light, then send this light to those who you hold dear and see them immersed in the light for their highest good. See the earth bathed in the light, a golden ball of light, and ask that peace and harmony will come to earth.

Gradually the white light turns to pink and you see the rose in the garden of roses. Inhale again its fragrance and give thanks for that which you have received. Walk down the pathway on which you came and as you pass the roses of many colours see if there is one that catches your eye. Make a note of the colour for it could be very meaningful. Walk through the gate and down the steps, then take a deep breath and before opening your eyes see yourself in a white cloak of light. Close your chakra centres, move your hands and feet and then open your eyes. If you wish, look up the attributes of the colour you saw and find its meaning.

THE INNER TEMPLE

We all long for security and a feeling that we know all our needs are met. God is love and we live in a world of abundance, and yet so many have little while others have so much. The spiritual laws are just and as we have sown in the past so we reap in the present. When we find that we lack the needs of life, then we should give as much as we can to others and think less about our needs. That way wonderful events start to happen in our lives. Think of these things as we enter the next meditation.

Relax and breathe deeply, close your eyes and ask that you be protected while you enter the silence, that the white light will enfold and protect you for your highest good. Focus your attention on your brow centre and see yourself sitting under a tree. Its branches are big and broad and reach up to the sky; it's a warm and sunny day and you have light clothing on and no shoes.

In front of you is a stream and you get up and walk towards it; you step into the water to paddle and find that the water is warm and there is a slight current which washes over your feet. Looking upstream, you see a waterfall and decide to walk towards it. You enter the waterfall, knowing that you are safe, and as you do you suddenly feel lighter. The water has a purifying effect and it makes your skin tingle. You can see the sun's rays pouring through the water and all the colours of the rainbow pour over you, they glisten in the sunlight, you glow all over and feel alive, uplifted, renewed, rejuvenated. The water feels warm with the sun's rays pouring on it and all aches and pains vanish, all tension and worries leave you. Continue to feel the water pour over you as you stay for a while.

Now step out to the other side of the waterfall. You realize you have a robe of blue around you, tinged with gold. Ahead of you is a mountain and you feel drawn to walk towards it. As you approach, a being of great light approaches you — it is your teacher, mentor and friend. Thank him for all the help you have received. You may ask your teacher about your life — listen to the answer and stay a while. Feel the presence of God's love and light pour into you from this beautiful being. You are now ready to ascend the mountain: you may be given a candle, or a book or a few words of advice. Remember what happens for it is important for you.

As you begin your ascent, to begin with it is tiring and then you realize you have only to think yourself to the top and you are there. In front of you is the most beautiful temple you have ever seen: it has a golden dome and the walls shimmer with all the colours. You stand in awe. There is music coming from the temple and several steps lead up to an archway whereby you can enter. The music from within is like food for your soul and in the middle is a golden light. Walk towards the light and bathe yourself in this light. You now realize the purpose and meaning of your life, the lessons to be learned, and an understanding of life and events become clear to you. You relax more and more, the colour and music fill and enfold you, giving you as much healing as you can accept. Feel it pour into you and know that you are part of God, linked to his abundance, and that from now on all your needs are met. Share this abundance with those you meet for it is an eternal spring. The child within you sings with joy: from now on you know your heavenly Father protects you and guides you and feeds you. Be aware of it and give thanks for that which you have received in the temple.

The time has come for you to leave the temple of light but remember you can visit again any time you like. Start to descend the mountain and soon you are once again at the bottom; take leave of your guide, friend and mentor and very slowly walk back towards the stream. As you get nearer to the stream you see there are stepping stones to cross over to the other side, and when you reach the other side you see you are again dressed in your own clothing. Sit down once again under the tree and look back at the mountain: it is now shrouded in mist but it is a place you can go at any time to visit your inner temple where you and God are one. Imagine a cloak of light around you and close your chakra centres, take some deep breaths, and open your eyes.

__ THE FOUNTAINS OF COLOUR __

Make sure you surround yourself with the white light before entering the silence, take some deep breaths and relax as you breathe out. Say to yourself 'I am relaxing more and more', and close your eyes. Centre your attention on your brow centre and see in front of you a lake; in the centre of this lake are several fountains pouring out water in all the colours of the rainbow — they are a magnificent sight to see — and as you walk round the lake you come across a bridge that will take you to the fountains. When you reach the island in the centre you feel very light, as though all heaviness that you had has left you. You look up at the sunlight and feel the warmth of the rays of the sun pour into you.

The first fountain you come to is pouring out all the colours, the fountain of life. As you step inside your whole being tingles and you feel refreshed. The red ray gives you strength, the orange ray brings you vitality, the golden yellow ray feeds you with ideas and the blue rays cool and calm you down and link you with higher ideals. You notice a cup near the fountain and you decide to take a drink of water from the cup. As this goes into you, a feeling of well-being comes over you that you have never felt before; it's as though the spirit of life is within you and you are renewed. Every part of you comes to life, a new life; you are aware of opportunities that await you and you have a feeling of dancing with joy within yourself. After a while you step out and walk on.

The next fountain is pouring out all the greens you can imagine, tinged with gold. As you step inside the fountain, you have a feeling of eternal youth, new beginnings, and your whole being is uplifted. The emerald ray rejuvenates and regenerates your entire being; the pale apple green links you to the brotherhood of man, our link with each other, and your heart opens in thanksgiving for all you have and all you are. The golden yellow illuminates your mind with wonderful ideas and as you drink from the cup all the past has gone so that only the present remains. Your heart becomes filled with love and light until it overflows and after a while you step out and walk on.

The next fountain that you see is all the blues, from royal to purple to amethyst and they are all tinged with gold. Walk towards it, step inside and drink from the cup of these divine colours. The healing rays of God pour through you, clearing away all the dross of the past and giving deeper insight into who you are and why you are here. Your whole being vibrates more quickly and you have a feeling of being at one with all that is. Everyone longs for peace, for harmony in their lives; the blue ray is giving you all of this and healing all aspects of yourself. Your faith and trust is renewed to the extent that you can accept this experience for, as we think, so it is. When you are ready, step out and walk on.

And so you walk back to the fountain of life and bathe once again in the waters, taking from the cup of many colours and, feeling now enlightened and refreshed, you gradually walk back to the bridge. Before stepping over the bridge, ask what colour would help you at this time, make a note of it and use it, for it can transform you and lift you to new heights of awareness that you have not thought of. You have around you the robe of many colours, for you have been bathed in the colours of light. Go forth, giving the light and the love that you have received, bring a smile and some joy to others, help others to become aware that we are all light beings. Be aware of your cloak of many colours, close your centres and ask the light to protect, guide and bless you for your highest good. When you are ready, open your eyes.

You can say after each meditation the following: 'I ask the light to fill, enfold, surround and protect me for my highest good. Amen.'

REFERENCES

Alder, Vera Stanley, *The Finding of the Third Eye*, Rider, 1987.

Aivanhov, Omraam Mikhael, *The Second Birth*; *The Splendour of Tipheret*, *Light is a Living Spirit, Man's Subtle Bodies and Centres*; all Editions Prosveta.

Bek, Lilla, and Pullar, Philippa, *The Seven Levels of Healing*, Rider, 1986; *To the Light*, Allen & Unwin, 1985.

Babbitt, Edwin S., *Light, Colour and the Environment*, Van Nostrand Reinhold Co., 1969.

Gimbel, Theo, *Sound, Colour and Healing*; *Healing Through Colour*, C. W. Daniel Co., 1980.

Haich, Elisabeth, *Initiation*, Seed Center, 1974.

Hunt, Roland, *The Seven Keys to Colour Healing*, C. W. Daniel Co., 1963.

Kilner, Walter J., *The Human Atmosphere*, University Books, New York.

Leadbeater, C. W., *Man Visible, Invisible*, Theosophical Publishing House, 1975.

Ouseley, S. G. J., *The Science of the Aura*, L. N. Fowler & Co., 1949.

HOW TO USE THE
COLOUR KEYS

THE COLOUR KEYS

There are 28 colour cards in the pack which are known as Colour Keys — seven cards are all one colour, five cards have a clear top with a colour below, and 16 cards show dual colours.

PREPARATION FOR USE OF THE COLOUR KEYS

Red   Red placed on top of another colour means you have a strong will but you need to look at your motives, except when over violet, in which case your life is one of service to others.

Pink   When pink is above you are very sensitive; when the pink is below you have a lot of love to give but are not expressing it.

Orange   When this colour is over a cool colour (blue, indigo or violet) you are not expressing how you truly feel and think; you are blocking your own good and the colour below needs to be released (refer to the colour and its attributes).

Yellow   This colour is linked to mind. When it is over a cool colour (except in the spiritual realm) you are letting your mind dominate your life. When this colour is on top in the spiritual realm it denotes wisdom.

Green   The colour relating to space and balance. When this colour is below you need space, when it is above you have much to give and have an open heart. (When this colour is above one of the cool colours — blue, indigo or violet — they are in the wrong order, suggesting that you are seeing life in the wrong perspective — see note below.)

Blue   When this colour is on top you are using your intuition, you love peace and beauty. When it is below you are ignoring the deeper issues of your life.

Violet   When this colour is on top there is a tendency to use your power for your own aggrandizement. You can be eccentric and easily become depressed. When the colour is below you have transmuted lower desires for a higher ideal.

Note: The order of the colours, from slow to fast vibration, are: red, orange, yellow, green, blue, indigo, violet. Where a slower vibration is above a faster vibration in your reading, you are looking at life with an inverted perspective — except where indicated.

THE FOUR REALMS

Physical Realm   A lack of reds in this realm can mean one needs more energy, one is too lethargic (see information on the red ray and its positive attributes). No orange means a lack of confidence and the need to express yourself more.

Emotional Realm   Too many yellows indicate an intellectual approach to life. Too many reds suggest you are inclined to be over-emotional.

Mental Realm   Too many yellows show an analytical approach to life. A lot of red here would suggest you can be overbearing.

Spiritual Realm   No blue or violet indicates a person who has a limited awareness of life, from a spiritual point of view, and needs to use more intuition.

When reading the information for the different realms below, the colours on the right are recommended for you to work with, either breathing in the colour or using solarized water, or just being aware of the colours, and you will start to attract it and its attributes.

Note that the information given here for the different colour rays are guidelines. When you have studied them for some time you will be able to add to what I have given here, out of your own insight, and therefore KNOW YOURSELF as you have never known yourself before.

READINGS WITH
—————— THE COLOUR KEYS ——————

THE MAIN READING

1. Shuffle the cards and cut three times.
2. Place the cards in four rows of seven, face downwards, placing from left to right.
First row: Spiritual Realm.
Second row: Emotional Realm.
Third row: Mental Realm.
Fourth row: Physical Realm.
3. Turn the cards over, *making sure you do not turn them round as this will alter which colour appears above the other.*
4. Refer to the reference below for each card and read it accordingly, linking the card to the realm. For example, if the card is placed in the third row, look up what it says for the Mental Realm.
5. Wherever the indigo card has been placed is important, for that indicates the focus for you at the time. The two cards either side of the indigo card should also be noted for they could be highly relevant at this time.
6. Start with the indigo card and read that realm first, then continue reading the rest of the cards.

SHORT READING

1. Shuffle the cards and cut three times.
2. Choose three cards from anywhere in the pack and place face downwards, as shown.

Card one indicates how you are at the moment, what energies you have and are using.
Card two indicates the inner aspect of yourself.
Card three should link with the first card to give some indication of how you are progressing into the future. If it does not relate to the first card, pick another one, for you may be blocking your own good. You

may shuffle them again and, holding the cards, ask them to help you to know how you are progressing, or how you should proceed, then pick one from the pack face down.

Read the cards for every realm: physical, emotional, mental, and spiritual.

THE TRIANGLE READING

1. Shuffle the cards and cut three times.
2. Place the cards in a triangular shape, as shown, and make sure in turning the cards over you do not turn them round, for that will alter the reading. Cards 5, 8 and 9, being the inner part of the triangle, show the inner you while 1 is your focus. Cards 2, 3, 4, 6, 7 and 10 are your outer expression.

Example:

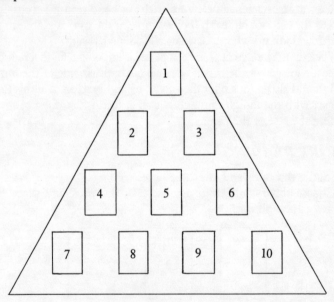

Focus

Card 1. Green over green — Interested in nature and love the outdoors, you can give to the detriment of yourself. You love animals and children, and possessions are important to you. You need space and the right environment to live in. You can start many things and see them come to fruition. You have understanding and sympathy for others and are adaptable and can discriminate.

Your Inner Self

Card 5. Clear space over yellow — You can be wise. Space and balance are important to you.

Card 8. Blue over green — Surroundings are important to you. You long for peace in all your affairs; you have a decision to make of the heart. At present you feel hemmed in, try to forget yourself and think more of others. Count your blessings.

Card 9. Yellow over yellow — Thinking too much of yourself. You have a good mind and ideas flow to you; basically a sunny nature, warm and friendly but you need to be loved for yourself. Others feel good in your presence.

Your Outer Expression

Card 2. Violet over blue — Can become depressed easily and appear aloof and distant; a wonderful creative mind. You are aware you have a mission to accomplish but you are not using your wisdom deep inside yourself.

Card 3. Red over green — Too focused on your family and immediate environment; expand your awareness and think of others. A romantic at heart, you have a strong masculine energy. This applies whether you are a man or woman; a woman would need to be more receptive and feminine. The green at the base is a longing for space.

Card 4. Orange over green — Use your power of thought positively and this will help you to change your life. Usually you are very sociable and like being the centre of attention but deep down you are insecure. Others feel better when you are around, you have a sense of warmth and fun, but you need your own space to be yourself at the moment. You can be an extrovert or introvert, depending on how you feel.

Card 6. Violet over violet — Very creative, love the arts and have much potential; you have a reverence for all life, and you will let nothing stand in the way of what you think is right for you to do.

Card 7. Blue over yellow — You are at a turning point in your life. Do not block your own good; ask for guidance. You cope well in difficult circumstances. Do not take life too seriously; find the balance and allow the wisdom deep inside you to express itself.

Card 10. Orange over blue — At the moment you have turned to more social activities and you are suppressing your finer feelings. Release the emotions; life at the moment seems empty.

An Overview
This person needs the blue ray of trust and faith, and to realize they have access to much wisdom within although, at the moment, feeling lost as they face a crossroads in their life. They have much creativity and should use it as they would find it very therapeutic. There is a need here for space to think everything over — emotional decisions will always cloud the mind and this is why they are not thinking clearly at present. A change of scenery would help and using the power of positive thinking would change their attitudes and approach. They have become introspective and need to see a balance, so the green ray would help at this time.

—— THE SEVEN COLOUR RAYS ——

————— THE RED RAY —————

THE SPIRIT OF LIFE

Affirmation I am strong and full of courage and succeed in all I do.
Expression The red ray gives us energy and strength. When we are listless and feel run down this ray will recharge our energies. It is the ray of love in all its aspects. We need to forgive ourselves as this stops many from enjoying their lives to the full. Being unforgiving colours our perceptions — forgive others and we are forgiven for our past mistakes as well. We need to have the courage of our convictions, and the will to succeed in all we undertake. When white is introduced into the red ray we have the pink ray of unconditional love. This is the love that heals, unites and releases the past.

Attributes of the Red Ray

Positive	Negative
Courageous	Dominant
Determined	Resentful
Truthful	Sentimental
Strong willed	Self pitying
Spontaneous	Obstinate
Grateful	Quick tempered

Forgiving	Violent
Perseverant	Ruthless
	Passionate
	Brutal

Visualize: A red rose or any red flower, a red sunset with its many different hues. Breathe in the colour.

THE PINK RAY

Affirmation I love others and I am loved.
Expression Unconditional love.

Attributes of the Pink Ray: Love, kindness, gentleness, serving for the sake of serving, loving unconditionally.

Visualize: Pink roses or pink carnations. Breathe in the colour.
Some Tints and Shades — Guidelines as to their meanings.
Wine: The colour of purification.
Magenta: Spiritually uplifting.
Brown: Growth and effort, but can link one too much to security patterns.

THE ORANGE RAY

THE SPIRIT OF HEALTH

Affirmation I release joy within; I feel alive and well.
Expression As we think, so we are. Orange is linked to health and vitality; to think pure thoughts and have a certain amount of exercise. Joy is an expression from deep within one's being, it is not subject to outer circumstances, it radiates and brings life to everything. This is the colour of creativity and our outer expression of being. We all need joy, it holds the energy of love and wisdom, having red (love) and yellow (wisdom) within it. Children who have a lot of orange in their aura mature early; it is the ray of confidence and independence.

Attributes of the Orange Ray	
Positive	*Negative*
Joyous	Despondent

Self-confident	Proud
Enthusiastic	Exhibitionist
Independent	Sloth
Sociable	Leans on others
Constructive	Destructive

Visualize: A marigold or an orange (fruit) or any flower that is this colour.
Breathe in the colour.
Some Tints and Shades — Guidelines as to their meanings
Peach: Creative expression.
Apricot: Love of beauty.
Salmon pink: A sense of well-being, and love of life.
Note: Ambition is an attribute of this ray. We need golden orange so that the energy is for everyone and not so much for the self. The gold links us to the higher wisdom.

THE YELLOW RAY

THE SPIRIT OF KNOWLEDGE AND WISDOM

Affirmation Ideas flow to me; I feel renewed.
Expression This ray brings clarity of thought, ideas and an expansion of awareness. One must be careful not to become too studious and analytical, for life is synthesis and unity. The golden yellow ray is linked to wisdom — wise in thought, word and deed. A wise person usually says little but when they do say something it is meaningful.

Attributes of the Yellow Ray

Positive	Negative
Awareness	Analytical
Good humour	Likes flattery
Broad mind	Exaggerates
Wide field of interests	Shrewd
Optimistic	Devious
Confident	Feels inferior
Good discernment	Can be vindictive
Clear logical mind	Pessimistic
	Cowardly

Visualize: A field of golden yellow daffodils. Feel as though you are walking amongst them, and breathe in the colour.
Some Tints and Shades — Guidelines as to their meanings.
Bright Yellow: A sunny nature and a person who has a lot of confidence.
Pale Yellow: A good mind, the philosopher and seeker after truth.
Mustard Yellow: Very analytical, argumentative, can be vindictive.
Golden Yellow: The colour of wisdom with knowledge.

THE GREEN RAY

THE SPIRIT OF EVOLUTION

Affirmation I feel young and free. My life is just beginning.
Expression Green is linked to sympathy, compassion and understanding others' needs. This colour is associated with abundance and plenty, those who love green are the great givers of our universe. Make sure you do not give to the detriment of yourself. Green is linked to money, which is energy, and it is a question of what we do with that energy, for as we give so we receive. We talk about green fingers — plants thrive under their care. They love children and the home is important. Green is to do with self-esteem and how we think of ourselves and others. The lighter greens are associated with unity and brotherhood.

Attributes of the Green Ray	
Positive	*Negative*
Political and industrial reformers	Lack of judgement
	Unscrupulous with money
Sympathy and compassion	Indifferent
Harmony	Miserly
Understanding	Hang onto possessions
Adaptable	Envious and jealous
Discriminating	
Self-control	
Love children and animals	

Visualize: Walking in a wood at springtime, the energy rises within you, as it does within the trees and all nature. You feel young and as though your life is just beginning — each day is a new day. Breathe in the green ray.
Some Tints and Shades — Guidelines as to their meanings.

Light Greens: Sympathy and compassion.
Deep Grass Green: Strength and a feeling of well-being.
Very Dark Greens: Envy and jealousy.

——————— THE BLUE RAY ———————

THE SPIRIT OF TRUTH

Affirmation I feel at peace, and inspiration flows to me.
Expression This colour is linked to faith and trust, integrity and devotion, it gives one a sense of beauty. Music and the arts are important to you. Blue is the ray of the soul's purpose for incarnating at this time. It is a great healing ray and brings peace and direction. While our lives are in turmoil we feel lost.

Attributes of the Blue Ray

Positive	*Negative*
Loyalty	Ambitious
Trust	Unfaithful
Faith	Lack of trust
Integrity	Separateness
Serenity	Superstitious
Tactfulness	Apathetic
Inventiveness	Self-righteous
Inspiration	Snobbish
Devotion	Emotionally unstable
	Aloof and distant

Visualize: A field of bluebells, or blue hyacinths, irises etc. When they are in flower their fragrance will purify an atmosphere and lift one's vibration. Breathe in the colour.
Some Tints and Shades — Guidelines as to their meanings.
Royal Blue: Loyalty, power and high ideals.
Navy Blue: Good judgement.
Very Dark Blue: Too set in one's ideas, think one knows everything.
Pale Blue: Very spiritual colour, serve for the sake of serving.

THE INDIGO RAY

THE SPIRIT OF INTUITION AND POWER

Affirmation I am a teacher, and teach by example.

Expression The great searcher after the truth, 'Why am I here?' 'What is life all about?' There is a saying 'As we seek, we shall find.' Once we get in touch with this vibration we understand some of the causes behind form, and the meaning of life opens up before us. It teaches us, among other things, the great law of acceptance, to accept the things we cannot change. It is interesting that when we accept a situation and let go, marvellous things start to happen in our lives. A person who is in tune with this vibration can awaken others to their true potential. It is a scientific ray and with it goes much power, but one needs the golden yellow ray of wisdom and knowledge to go with it. Teach by example and heal by your presence.

Attributes of the Indigo Ray

Positive	*Negative*
Highly intuitive	Separateness
Faith	Fearful
Sense of unity	Intolerant
Fearless	Impractical
Reformers	Judgemental
Devotion to duty	Inconsiderate
Articulate	Scattered mind
Orderly mind	Sees only the black side
Practical idealists	Depressed easily
Very active in their environment	

Visualize: The sky at midnight, a deep, deep blue. Breathe in the colour.

Some Tints and Shades — Guidelines as to their meanings.

When black is introduced into indigo they can be very dictatorial, lacking tolerance and understanding. The true hue of this colour is linked to practical idealism and one must find a way to serve humanity.

THE VIOLET RAY

THE SPIRIT OF SACRIFICE

Affirmation I sacrifice my life to a higher ideal; I have power and use it wisely.

Expression Violet is power and needs to be used wisely. When it is used for the self it will backfire, so it needs to be used in the service of others — serve for the sake of serving. It is the ray of higher aspiration, in music and the arts or to work for a high ideal. When it is linked to the golden yellow ray of wisdom, life stands before you and you know a joy and peace others are not aware of.

Attributes of the Violet Ray

Positive	Negative
Transmutation of desire	Flaunt their power
A reverance for all life	Think they are superior
Outstanding in their jobs	Arrogant
Great mental powers	Snobbish
Inspired leaders	Faithless
Kind and just	No concern for others
Humanitarians	Fanatics
Self-sacrifice	Treacherous
Pure idealism	Morbid interest in Black Magic and mysticism

Visualize: Violets. Also, lilac with its fragrance has wonderful healing energies. Breathe in the colour.

Some Tints and Shades — Guidelines as to their meanings.

Pure Violet: High spiritual qualities, with strong psychic abilities.

Dark Violet: Power to control others for selfish reasons.

Purple: Power of eloquence over many; needs the golden yellow of wisdom to act as a balance.

Lavender: Very healing and spiritual colour.

Amethyst: High ideals, devotion and loyalty.

INTERPRETING
——— THE COLOUR KEYS ———

——— CLEAR COLOURS ———

The clear space above indicates clarity to the colour below.

Pink   Unconditional love, a need to be loved for yourself.
Green   Harmony with your surroundings is important — a new beginning for you.
Blue   Peace is important to you, use your intuition.
Yellow   Use the wisdom within yourself. Space and balance needed here.
Violet   A dedication of one's life to serve the whole; quite often the pioneer.

When the clear space is below the colour the meanings are as follows.

Pink   A need for loving relationships around you.
Green   You need space, peace and harmony.
Blue   Looking for your direction.
Yellow   You have a good mind but need wisdom in your affairs.
Violet   You have much potential and creativity — use it.

——— SINGLE COLOURS ———

PHYSICAL REALM

Red   You are earthed and practical; a sexual relationship is important to you.
Orange   Sociable, outgoing by nature. Sports, yoga, or some form of exercise is also important to you. Watch your diet.
Yellow   Rather self-centred; a lack of awareness.
Green   Interested in nature at every level, loves the outdoors.
Blue   Introspection, the perfectionist.
Indigo   Appearances are important to you: go deeper within, there is more to life than it would appear.
Violet   Use your creativity to beautify your surroundings.

EMOTIONAL REALM

Red   Sentimental, can be possessive.

Orange   Family relationships are important to you.

Yellow   A sunny nature, warm and friendly, but deep inside a need to be loved for yourself.

Green   You can give to the detriment of yourself; you always have an open house; you are a lover of animals and children; possessions are important to you.

Blue   Hypersensitive, for self and others.

Indigo   You care for others, a need here to work in one of the caring professions. If not you will get very frustrated.

Violet   You will let nothing stand in the way of what you think is right for you to do; you can easily get depressed. Unpredictable; love beautiful things.

MENTAL REALM

Red   You have courage, strength and determination to succeed.

Orange   A mental ray. You are a good communicator. What you think, you attract, whether purity, security, prosperity or the negative aspect of these.

Yellow   An ideas person, you will always be able to earn your living. Beware of becoming too studious, analytical or too introverted. You need to cultivate a broad and logical mind and have a wide field of interests.

Green   Peace and balance are important to you, you need space and the right environment. You have the capacity to start many things and see them through to fruition.

Blue   You have a good mind and can be very inventive. Beware of peace at any price.

Indigo   You are a searcher after truth, have a need to find the meaning and purpose of life; you can be highly intuitive and have the ability to influence others.

Violet   Very artistic and creative; loves music and the arts in any form. Tune into the higher aspect of self and you will bring through new creations.

SPIRITUAL REALM

Red   Make sure you are using this power ray to help others —

rededicate your life to serve a high ideal. To move energy in a positive way.

Orange Purity of thought, word and deed is important to you. You have a sense of joy, are warm hearted and your enthusiasm encourages others.

Yellow In the spiritual realm this denotes much wisdom through lessons learned in the past.

Green You have sympathy and true understanding for others, you are adaptable and can discriminate.

Blue You are highly intuitive, a lover of music, you see beauty in all forms.

Indigo You have power with much knowledge, use it wisely. Having searched for the meaning and purpose of life, through life's experiences your consciousness expands and the true meaning of life dawns within you. A teacher and a knower of the inner mysteries, you realize that life on earth is a school, teaching the knowledge of the heavens.

Violet You have reverence for all life and access to great mental powers.

DUAL COLOURS

	Spiritual realm	Recommended colours
Violet over Blue	You are aware you have a mission to fulfil, but you are blocking your own good and need the yellow of wisdom to go forward.	**Gold/ Yellow**
Blue over Violet	You have a peace and presence which helps others to feel better, you are a teacher and a healer.	**Gold/ Yellow**
	Mental realm	
Violet over Blue	Very creative mind, you need stimulus, mix with more people who share the same interests, do not live alone at the present unless you cannot avoid it. You need golden yellow to brighten your days.	**Gold/ Yellow**

		Recommended colours
Blue over Violet	You give and serve without thought of self.	**Gold/ Yellow**

Emotional realm

Violet over Blue	You get depressed and do not know why — you need pink to warm and relax you; you can appear aloof and distant.	**Orange, Pink**
Blue over Violet	Allow others to do things for you, you have to learn to receive as well as give. You need to be fed emotionally, spiritually and mentally.	**Orange, Indigo**

Physical realm

Violet over Blue	You need yellow to bring out a sunny nature; you can be very subdued.	**Yellow**
Blue over Violet	You are a real dedicated soul; be kind to yourself. Discipline is good for the soul but one needs joy as well.	**Orange**

Spiritual realm

Violet over Pink	The pink ray of love needs releasing; you are rather obsessed with your own problems; help others and your life will change.	**Pink**
Pink over Violet	You are aware you have a deep mission to accomplish. A child or adult who picks this card is aware of the spiritual world and that as we ask for guidance, we receive it.	**Indigo**

Mental realm

Violet over Pink	You soon get frustrated, you need yellow for divine ideas.	**Yellow**
Pink over Violet	You have the ability to awaken others to a greater understanding of the world. Find your way, ask in prayer and it will be revealed to you.	**Gold/ Yellow**

		Recommended
	Emotional realm	colours
Violet **over** **Pink**	You have so much love to give; love others and it will come back to you a thousand fold. You bottle up your emotions — release them.	**Orange,** **Pink**
Pink **over** **Violet**	Over-sensitive and mediumistic, there is a need here to protect the aura; you give a lot of love, but need to be loved.	**Pink/** **Gold/** **Yellow**

Physical realm

Violet **over** **Pink**	Very creative, the artist, sculptor, designer, musician. Use the creativity otherwise you will stagnate and be very unhappy.	**Orange/** **Blue**
Pink **over** **Violet**	You love beauty in all shape and form, and see beauty where others do not see it, you are aware of the divine seed in all creation.	**Green,** **Blue**

Spiritual realm

Blue **over** **Green**	You have a lot to give, but have a feeling of being hemmed in. Help others and forget yourself — your life will open up.	**Green,** **Orange**
Green **over** **Blue**	Stand up and be counted; think of pink and orange. You need warmth and the feeling that you are loved.	**Pink,** **Orange,** **Blue**

Mental realm

Blue **over** **Green**	These two colours can often mean there is a decision to be made about a relationship, for the green is linked to the heart, and the blue brings healing.	**Gold/** **Yellow**
Green **over** **Blue**	You need time to think everything over; have a change of scenery, it could change your perspective. Tendency to be pessimistic.	**Orange,** **Blue**

Emotional realm

Blue **over** **Green**	A longing for peace in all your affairs.	**Green,** **Blue**

		Recommended colours
Green over Blue	You get depressed easily; you need the pink of love to warm your heart.	**Pink, Green, Blue**

Physical realm

Blue over Green	Your surroundings are important to you; a need here for parks and open spaces.	**Green**
Green over Blue	You need a change, you are not happy with your present situation.	**Green, Yellow**

Spiritual realm

Blue over Red	You are strong spiritually; others will lean on you, help them find their own inner guidance.	**Gold/ Yellow**
Red over Blue	You have a strong will. Pray God's will be done through you and release the Blue.	**Blue**

Mental realm

Blue over Red	You have the capacity to bring your ideas to fruition.	**Gold/ Yellow**
Red over Blue	Your intuition is blocked, tune into the blue ray, be careful you do not become overbearing, be open to others' points of view.	**Gold/ Yellow, Blue**

Emotional realm

Blue over Red	A good balance of energy here, you have strong emotions, make sure you channel them into the right area. Can be very intuitive.	**Violet, Indigo**
Red over Blue	You need your feet on the ground, you can soon become emotional, particularly if things do not suit you; you react quickly and regret afterwards.	**Green, Blue**

	Physical realm	**Recommended colours**
Blue over Red	A definite personality, you know where you are going.	**Green, Blue**
Red over Blue	You tend to dominate others; this is caused by a lack of confidence in yourself.	**Orange, Blue**

	Spiritual realm	
Blue over Yellow	Allow the wisdom deep inside you to express itself.	**Gold/ Yellow**
Yellow over Blue	Here yellow is gold, you have integrity and can be trusted as a friend indeed.	**Violet**

	Mental realm	
Blue over Yellow	You are highly intuitive, but to earth your ideas you need to use the yellow; you are inclined to be too ethereal and not earthed.	**Yellow**
Yellow over Blue	The mind here overrules the intuition; think blue and you will find a balance through the green ray. You need to make up your mind about an important decision.	**Green, Blue**

	Emotional realm	
Blue over Yellow	You cope well in difficult situations, the real stoic, a tendency here to take life too seriously. You need orange, the ray of joy, and this will release the yellow.	**Orange/ Yellow**
Yellow over Blue	You suppress your deeper aspects; watch your health, the golden yellow of wisdom will help here and open a door to you. Do not become a martyr.	**Gold/ Yellow**

		Recommended colours
	Physical realm	
Blue over Yellow	You are at a turning point in your life, do not block your own good. Pray and ask for guidance — as we seek, so we shall find; as we knock on the door, so it shall be opened.	**Gold/ Yellow**
Yellow over Blue	Do not ignore the body, look after it, otherwise you will regret it later. The yellow of the mind gets so caught up in studious things that the self forgets the physical body.	**Orange/ Blue**
	Spiritual realm	
Yellow over Pink	Ask for the meaning of divine wisdom and divine love, then you will know the truth. The yellow here is wisdom, the pink is love.	**Pink, Yellow, Blue**
Pink over Yellow	Here the pink has risen up and it is in an outpouring of love, like a rebirth — you start to see everything differently.	**Blue, Gold/ Yellow**
	Mental realm	
Yellow over Pink	The yellow here means a very open mind; you can appear tough, but inside you are a softie.	**Gold/ Yellow**
Pink over Yellow	Very vulnerable, others try to override you.	**Orange/ Blue**
	Emotional realm	
Yellow over Pink	Love for greater knowledge and understanding of life, you have a quest for the purpose and meaning of life. You have much love to give.	**Indigo, Pink**
Pink over Yellow	A lovely nature but you tend to be naïve. You need the golden yellow of wisdom.	**Gold/ Yellow**
	Physical realm	
Yellow over Pink	Opening to a greater awareness of what life is all about.	**Yellow, Green**

Recommended
colours

Pink   You do not know yourself — release the yellow   **Yellow**
over   of mind and you will surprise yourself.
Yellow

Spiritual realm

Red   You are only concerned with your immediate   **Gold/**
over   family and environment; expand your aware-   **Yellow**
Green   ness to a greater whole.

Green   Balance and harmony are important to you,   **Orange,**
over   you have a love of open spaces and you love   **Blue**
Red   life and all it represents.

Mental realm

Red   You are focused too much on yourself, here   **Orange,**
over   indicated by the red ray. Start to think of   **Blue**
Green   others.

Green   Good business mind and aware of others'   **Blue**
over   needs and you do something about it.
Red

Emotional realm

Red   You are a romantic, your sex life is mainly in   **Blue**
over   the imagination, and does not come up to
Green   expectations.

Green   You are very vulnerable and easily hurt, any   **Blue**
over   sexual relationship needs to be one of deep
Red   love.

Physical realm

Red   The red on top indicates a strong use of   **Gold/**
over   masculine energy; this is fine for a man, but   **Yellow,**
Green   when the red ray is on top for a woman, she   **Green**
   is using too much of the masculine energy,
   and she will find she is left to do everything
   herself and wondering why. The green at the
   base is a longing for space.

		Recommended colours
Green over Red	A good balance of energy for a woman, the green here is the feminine aspect of self; in the case of a man he is too feminine and needs to stand up for himself. It would also indicate a very sensitive man who, from red on the bottom, needs more strength.	**Gold/ Yellow**

Spiritual realm

Violet over Green	You are too introspective, very concerned with your own problems. Use your creativity, and meaning and purpose will return to your life.	**Orange/ Gold**
Green over Violet	You have brought your gifts back with you from the past, share them with mankind.	**Pink, Violet**

Mental realm

Violet over Green	You can be very melancholy at times, use the green ray to bring you out of yourself and remember the power of positive thinking.	**Gold/ Yellow, Green**
Green over Violet	The healer of the soul; help others to realize who they are, to uncover their potential and the purpose of life. A new beginning for you here.	**Gold/ Yellow**

Emotional realm

Violet over Green	Highly sensitive, your moods change quickly. It is important that you love what you do; there is a need here to use your creativity and this will bring you joy.	**Pink, Orange**
Green over Violet	The awakening of the soul and to one's destiny. You see beauty in all form; colour and music are important to you.	**Gold/ Yellow**

Physical realm

Violet over Green	A longing for space in which you are able to express your potential, you feel hemmed in. Find open spaces, get in touch with nature.	**Orange, Green**

		Recommended colours
Green over Violet	You have suffered much and now feel reborn, you have a new outlook on life, it is like a new beginning.	**Gold/ Yellow**

Spiritual realm

Green over Pink	A person who is very loving and caring but needs to show it and express it more.	**Orange, Pink**
Pink over Green	The pink here is the flowering of the true self, the two colours radiating from the heart centre. Spread love and peace.	**Green**

Mental realm

Green over Pink	Think of others and count your blessings.	**Orange, Blue**
Pink over Green	You long for space to be able to express your true self, you wish to be free of present circumstances — accept the situation and you will find your outer situations change.	**Orange, Green**

Emotional realm

Green over Pink	Open your heart to a greater understanding and your life will change, the greatest healer of this universe is love.	**Pink, Yellow**
Pink over Green	You know what it means to love unconditionally. Life's lessons have been hard, you can now help many on the pathway of life. You need space. You have a lot of love to give.	**Gold/ Yellow Blue, Green**

Physical realm

Green over Pink	People do not know you, as you hide behind your true self, and you need joy in your life.	**Orange**
Pink over Green	You wish to change what you are doing and/or your surroundings. Make your needs known and there could be changes.	**Green, Gold/ Yellow**

		Recommended
	Spiritual realm	colours
Blue **over** **Pink**	You are very intuitive and have much love to give. You have been very badly hurt in the past and tend not to show your feelings. Start to love more; express it and your life will change.	**Pink**
Pink **over** **Blue**	You identify with everyone's problems; protect your aura with the white light. It is important for you to live in the right environment. At times you can become over-emotional.	**Blue**

Mental realm

Blue **over** **Pink**	You have a good mind and can be very intuitive. You have the capacity to understand others' needs.	**Gold/** **Yellow**
Pink **over** **Blue**	You need strength of mind to stand up for yourself.	**Yellow**

Emotional realm

Blue **over** **Pink**	We are all God's children; you are the eternal mother, make sure you do not over-protect those near to you.	**Gold/** **Yellow**
Pink **over** **Blue**	You can be soft with others; you are easily hurt and people take advantage of you. The orange ray will give you confidence and strength.	**Orange**

Physical realm

Blue **over** **Pink**	Your life is hard but you accept it. Release the pink within, and start to have some fun in your life.	**Orange**
Pink **over** **Blue**	These two colours are complementary and yet both are receptive and emitting. Love is pink and faith and trust blue. Most people love these colours as they relate to the male and female aspects of the self; have trust and faith in what you do.	**Blue**

Recommended colours

Spiritual realm

Violet over Red	Great power over others — you need the gold yellow of wisdom. Power without wisdom will always destroy itself.	**Gold/ Yellow, Green**
Red over Violet	You have reverence for all life; you can tune into great spiritual power. Your life is one of service to others.	**Indigo, Pink, Gold– Yellow**

Mental realm

Violet over Red	You manipulate others to suit yourself — 'As we do unto others so are we done by', is a good saying to remember.	**Gold/ Yellow**
Red over Violet	This indicates you have dedicated your life to a higher ideal and to serving that ideal at all costs.	**Green, Pink**

Emotional realm

Violet over Red	Sexuality is important to you, but it must be beautiful and not obscene.	**Green, Pink**
Red over Violet	You have transmuted lower desires, and the red on top indicates you have sacrificed your lower self to find the higher self.	**Gold/ Yellow**

Physical realm

Violet over Red	You have it within you to make the earth more beautiful through your creativity and willingness to help others. Release the red within and you will succeed in all you do.	**Red, Gold/ Yellow**
Red over Violet	You have a lot of power — use it wisely.	**Gold/ Yellow**

		Recommended colours
Spiritual realm		
Yellow over Red	Yellow here is gold and links to wisdom. The red is strength; others will lean on you, help them find their own inner strength and wisdom.	**Gold/ Yellow, Violet**
Red over Yellow	You have everything in the wrong perspective and must rethink your life, your motives and where you are going. (For the slower vibration is above the faster, so the energy is the wrong way round.)	**Green, Gold/ Yellow**
Mental realm		
Yellow over Red	You have a powerful mind and project your own ideas onto another.	**Gold/ Yellow**
Red over Yellow	Think before you act or you could live to regret it. You can be overbearing at times.	**Pink, Gold/ Yellow**
Emotional realm		
Yellow over Red	You control your emotions but watch your health as you need to relax more.	**Blue**
Red over Yellow	You use your emotions to manipulate others.	**Gold/ Yellow, Pink**
Physical realm		
Yellow over Red	You have drive and energy for those things you are interested in.	**Green**
Red over Yellow	For you everything is black or white, there is no grey. You need a balance. You like to control your own and other people's lives as well but make sure it does not backfire.	**Green, Blue, Gold/ Yellow**

		Recommended colours

Spiritual realm

Green over Orange	You love harmony; release the joy within for you have much to give.	**Orange**
Orange over Green	Orange here is purity of thought, word and deed — use your power of thought to change your life. You long for peace in your life.	**Green, Yellow, Violet**

Mental realm

Green over Orange	Generous by nature, you have an understanding of other people's problems.	**Gold/ Yellow**
Orange over Green	Very sociable, you like being the centre of attention. You are a good communicator and have confidence in yourself.	**Green, Blue**

Emotional realm

Green over Orange	You care about people, are good with people and help to make them feel at ease, but you need more orange in your life. Don't take life too seriously.	**Orange, Blue**
Orange over Green	You often feel insecure, you need to balance the introvert and extrovert parts of yourself.	**Blue, Green**

Physical realm

Green over Orange	No discernment with money; give to the detriment of self; you need to understand the law of exchange. Green is energy and associated with money; balance is required here.	**Green, Gold/ Yellow**
Orange over Green	Others feel better when you are around; you have warmth and sense of fun, but the green also means space to be yourself.	**Green**

	Spiritual realm	Recommended colours
Blue over Orange	Become aware of your destiny. A searcher after truth.	**Indigo**
Orange over Blue	Life is empty. 'Seek and you will find' is a wonderful saying to keep in mind.	**Indigo, Pink**

	Mental realm	
Blue over Orange	You can take life too seriously; allow yourself some fun.	**Orange, Yellow**
Orange over Blue	At the moment life has to be lived at all costs, but at what expense? (Your true aspect of self lies buried so get in touch with your higher self, the blue.)	**Blue, Green**

	Emotional realm	
Blue over Orange	A good combination of energies; find the outer and inner balance; can be unpredictable; allow yourself to express your emotions as you tend to keep them bottled up.	**Pink, Green**
Orange over Blue	You suppress your finer feelings; at times you are fun, rather covering up your deeper feelings; watch your health.	**Blue, Green**

	Physical realm	
Blue over Orange	You like everything to look good, the perfectionist; be more flexible.	**Green**
Orange over Blue	More interested at the moment in social activities than deeper issues. All life needs a balance.	**Green**

	Spiritual realm	Recommended colours
Green over Yellow	You have a lovely nature — express it and release that sunny nature within.	**Yellow**
Yellow over Green	You long to be loved: as you love others, so you are loved. Do not analyse your relationships. At the moment you feel trapped.	**Pink**

	Mental realm	
Green over Yellow	Use your mind and be open to ideas; you allow others to influence you.	**Yellow**
Yellow over Green	You are very analytical. Expect a lot of changes in your life. You will always be able to earn your living. You have good ideas.	**Pink**

	Emotional realm	
Green over Yellow	The heart rules the mind.	**Gold/ Yellow**
Yellow over Green	The mind rules the heart. You have a decision to make about your emotions.	**Gold/ Yellow**

	Physical realm	
Green over Yellow	You need more activity in your life, you are too passive.	**Orange**
Yellow over Green	Find an objective and pursue it — you will do well. You need space.	**Orange**

	Spiritual realm	
Violet over Yellow	Reassess your life and decide where you are going.	**Gold/ Yellow, Blue**

		Recommended colours
Yellow over Violet	The yellow here is wisdom; you have dedicated your life to help mankind, you have a purpose and you are aware of the deeper meaning of life — follow your star.	**Pink**

Mental realm

Violet over Yellow	Release the yellow that links to mind; you have ideas but tend to bury them; you need the golden yellow of wisdom, then your life will change.	**Gold/ Yellow**
Yellow over Violet	You are a pioneer — bring in new discoveries and ideas to help mankind.	**Green, Gold/ Yellow**

Emotional realm

Violet over Yellow	You tend to identify with other people's problems and can be depressed. Strengthen your aura by picturing yourself in a beautiful golden light.	**Orange, Blue, Gold/ Yellow**
Yellow over Violet	Your past experiences help you to help others. the violet here means you have transmuted lower desires for a higher ideal.	**Pink, Green**

Physical realm

Violet over Yellow	You suppress the real you — stand up and be counted.	**Yellow, Blue**
Yellow over Violet	You have the ability to create artistic expressions.	**Pink, Yellow**

For more information and to find out who is your nearest colour therapist write to The International Association for Colour Therapy, 21 Portland Place, London W1 3AS, UK. For more information on the author's courses, write to BM Minuet, London WC1N 3XX.

INDEX

Aïvanhov, Omraam Mikhaël, 23
amethyst, 37
Ancient Greece, 11
antiseptics, 25
Aquarian Age, 13, 21, 30, 38
aura, 21, 22
aura-soma therapy, 54

Babbitt, Dr Edwin, 55
black, 20, 29, 42, 45
blue, Madonna, 38
blue, navy, 39, 74
blue ray, 38, 39, 46, 47, 48, 56, 57,
    65, 66, 68, 69, 73, 78, 80, 88, 99,
    101, 103, 104, 108, 122
blue, royal, 39
brain depressant, 41
Bristol Cancer Help Centre, 76
brown, 30

cancer patients, 53
Chromolight Filter Box, 52
church dignitaries, 36
Churchill, Winston, 36
clinics and schools, 47
colour affirmations, 68
colour and fear, 31
colour counsellor, 45
coloured candles, 56
colours and the people they can help,
    58
colours of the days, 56
colours of the spectrum, 31

complementary colours, 16
crystals and colour filters, 53

duality, 12

Egyptian civilization, 13
electromagnetic waves, 15
etheric aura, 24
Evening Primrose, 79

fashion world, 28
food in institutions, 78
Fraternité Blanche Universelle, 57, 66

gem remedy, 53
Gimbel, Theo, 48
green ray, 39, 40, 41, 47, 49, 50, 53,
    54, 57, 60, 65, 68, 69, 76, 79, 80,
    87, 98, 101, 108, 121

hospitals, 48
hydrotherapy pools, 49

indigo ray, 37, 46, 57, 62, 68, 69, 78,
    90, 97, 101, 123
inspirational work, 37

Kilner, Dr W.J., 19
Kirlian photography, 20, 55, 73

lavender, 37
Leadbeater, C.W., 20
Liaros, Carol Anne, 17

magenta, 17, 41, 42, 70
magnetized water, 51
Manners, Dr Peter Guy, 33
masters, the great, 21

Newton, Isaac, 11

Oldfield, Harry, 20
orange ray, 34, 35, 45, 53, 58, 68, 72,
  74, 76, 77, 79, 84, 98, 99, 119

Paracelsus, 11
past conditioning, 33
perfume manufacturers, 56
pink ray, 34, 35, 47, 48, 52, 53, 66,
  67, 70, 73, 103, 104, 105, 119
purifier, 37
purple, 35, 36
purple mantle, 37

ray of the soul, 38
red ray, 34, 35, 41, 47, 48, 56, 57, 58,
  68, 72, 76, 77, 79, 83, 97, 100, 109,
  118
respiration, 66

sacred dance, 33
salmon colour, 34
Schause, Dr, 47
school uniforms, 46
seven colours, 12

Seven Spirits, 25
silver ray, 31, 92
solarized water, 51
Soviet Union, 22
spirit of power, 37
Steiner, Rudolf (schools), 46
stones, 57

Thatcher, Margaret, 36
Theresa, Mother, 36
Trismegistus, Hermes, 40
turquoise, 46, 70

Victorians, 44
virtues, 24, 36
violet ray, 35, 41, 46, 48, 57, 63, 68,
  69, 80, 91, 98, 99, 100, 101, 124
da Vinci, Leonardo, 36

Wagner, 36
water, 65
wavelength and vibratory rate, 15
white, 47, 71
White Lodge, 38
winter months, 28

yellow, golden, 30, 94
yellow ray, 31, 32, 45, 48, 50, 56, 57,
  60, 68, 78, 79, 80, 85, 98, 99, 100,
  108, 120